PRAEGER LIBRARY OF U.S. GOVERNMENT DEPARTMENTS
AND AGENCIES

# The Department of Housing and Urban Development

PRAEGER LIBRARY OF U.S. GOVERNMENT DEPARTMENTS
AND AGENCIES

*Consulting Editors*

### Ernest S. Griffith

Former University Professor and Dean Emeritus, School of International Service, American University; former Director, Legislative Reference Service, Library of Congress; and author of *The American System of Government* and *The Modern Government in Action*

### Hugh Langdon Elsbree

Former Chairman, Department of Political Science, Dartmouth College; former Managing Editor, *American Political Science Review;* former Director, Legislative Reference Service, Library of Congress

# The Department of Housing and Urban Development

John B. Willmann

FREDERICK A. PRAEGER, *Publishers*
New York · Washington · London

FREDERICK A. PRAEGER, PUBLISHERS
111 Fourth Avenue, New York, N.Y. 10003, U.S.A.
77-79 Charlotte Street, London W.1., England

Published in the United States of America in 1967
by Frederick A. Praeger, Inc., Publishers

To my mother, Anna Catherine Willmann

# Preface

From almost the first day of its establishment in late 1965, the Department of Housing and Urban Development has been known, in the language of the nation's capital, by the simple, single-syllable name HUD. And by that name, rather than the spelled-out initials usually applied to federal government departments and agencies, it has become familiar across the country. The familiarity is both inevitable and heartening, for the Department called HUD deals in and with the problems of shelter and urban development that deeply concern all of us, as individuals and as citizens responsible to each other as neighbors.

In this fast-paced era of technological and scientific development, it is difficult for people to keep up with all that is happening. It can be even more difficult to understand how these events affect us and our daily lives. For this reason, public understanding of the nation's housing and urban programs, why they were developed, and how they are used by communities, is important. We all need to know what HUD is about.

This book has been written in an attempt to provide some background on the slowly developing recognition in Congress that we live in an urban age, worthy of a Cabinet department, and some idea of how the Department is organized and how it helps to plan, support, and participate in the building and rebuilding that must be done in urban areas to meet our ever-widening, complex needs. The descriptions of programs are contemporary—and subject to change in tomorrow's headlines.

As a journalist who has specialized in real estate and housing news in Washington, D.C., it has been my job for many
years to try to communicate to readers what is taking place in
the capital's own urban and suburban building programs, public and private. This book's larger examination of federal action in the related fields of residential housing and general
metropolitan development is partly an outcome of my professional interest in Washington's concern for what builders call
the "shelter industry."

From my own point of view, HUD can be regarded, most
interestingly, as having a mandate to provide all citizens, whatever their economic status, the opportunity to live in a digni-
fied residence—whether that means a modest mobile home, a
unit in a towering high-rise apartment building, or a house
owned outright, being purchased on a mortgage payment plan,
or rented from a corporate landlord. In this sense, the Department's main role can be seen as that of middleman (and catalyst) between a group including municipal leaders and those
who build residential shelter (or whole new cities) and another
group that includes citizens of meager or modest means who
need assistance in achieving their housing goals.

But HUD is much more, too. It is charged with responsibility for the rejuvenation of existing grubby neighborhoods, improvement of transportation facilities, stimulation of efforts for
more open space and beautification of existing public spaces,
and other action involving profound social changes. In many
cases, achieving all this, or part of it, means bettering the relationships between Washington and the nation's statehouses
and city halls.

Already, HUD has instituted hundreds of minor and major
study and experimental programs—the results of which we
may not be able to appraise fully for another ten years. This
book seeks to make no premature assessment of the Department as a whole, or of its programs. It does attempt to bring
together and, to some degree, analyze the backlog of federal
housing effort that preceded the Department itself; to describe

the elements pro and con involved in setting up the new federal entity; to outline the major roles set forth in the relevant legislation; and to look at the Department from within and without, seeking to find meaningful signs for the future.

In addition to the assistance offered freely by many members of the HUD team, during the preparation of this book I also had the benefit of the viewpoints and recollections of former federal officials, who willingly made themselves available for interviews. I have leaned heavily, too, on the files of *The Washington Post, The New York Times,* the *Christian Science Monitor, The Wall Street Journal,* and other papers in the course of writing these pages. A substantial part of the research and some of the writing and organization of the first draft were done by my oldest son, John Michael Willmann, a graduate of Fordham University. His contributions to a family-oriented undertaking were complemented by the typing assistance and prodding-to-work comments of my wife, Virginia, and our daughter, Ann.

*Washington, D.C.*
*June, 1967*                        JOHN B. WILLMANN

# Contents

# List of Maps and Charts

*A section of photographs follows page 82.*

# The Department of Housing and Urban Development

# I

# Before HUD

Where do you live?

Whether the answer to that question is Menlo Park, California; Cheyenne, Wyoming; Boston, Massachusetts; Perth Amboy, New Jersey; or Prince George's County, Maryland; for more and more Americans every year the meaning is the same: in an urban area, with problems.

In 1940, the proportion of people living in urban areas in the United States was 56 per cent. By 1950, it was 64 per cent. Today, the figure exceeds 70 per cent. Before this century ends, the urban population is expected to reach 280 million, with approximately 80 per cent of all Americans residing in metropolitan areas.

With this change in urban population has come a new responsibility for the federal government. It began in the Depression years of the 1930's with the necessity for emergency action in the housing field and led—tardily, in the view of studious observers—to the creation of the Department of Housing and Urban Development in late 1965.

Because the United States remained ideologically and politically rural long after the country way of life had been replaced by the urban way for great masses of people, Americans for many years were slow to recognize the need for governmental concern with rapidly multiplying urban problem areas. The relatively vigorous self-governments of cities for many decades kept their growing financial and other problems sufficiently in hand so that Congress remained unaware of the

3

trends in motion that eventually were to prove beyond the capacity of cities to handle. Then, even when the need to act was widely accepted, the nature of the representative system of government—state and federal—delayed response. Rural areas and populations were heavily overrepresented; state legislatures, in particular, showed little disposition either to enact policies in the interest of urban areas or to give urban areas the fiscal and other authority they required to act for themselves. Eventually, a proportionately heavy burden fell on the national government, which was catapulted into emergency housing action during the economic crisis of the 1930's.

Following the Depression and World War II, legislative response again failed to keep pace with the urgent needs arising from new housing and urban problems. The result, in the eyes of some observers, was further serious delay in taking steps to deal with these problems at the highest level of executive organization. To quote the somber comment of one scholar and former government official, Rufus E. Miles, Jr., in *Public Administration Review* of March, 1967:

> Two decades of urban decay, culminating in a series of social explosions, preceded recognition that the cities' problems deserved the kind of national attention and spotlight which accompanies Cabinet status. It will be remarkable and fortunate if, in the decade ahead, HUD is able to develop rapidly and imaginatively enough to overcome much of the damage done by this organization lag.

Housing and urban needs had so long been handled on a piecemeal basis, with federal legislation designed for each separate problem, that although, by the 1960's, the United States was dealing not with separate but with one interrelated urban problem, no over-all housing and urban program existed. When President John F. Kennedy and, later, President Lyndon B. Johnson, called on the Congress to establish a new department to deal with this need, urban disease already had a foothold. By the time the Congress approved President Johnson's bill to create the Department of Housing and Urban Development, it was unquestionably late in the day.

However, the new Department was, at least, set up in what seemed, to more optimistic viewers, a way that gave promise of working. HUD, as the Department quickly came to be called, was to channel its programs through communities, urban areas, states, and private and nonprofit sponsors, and to utilize loans, grants, mortgage insurance, and technical assistance of many kinds. By 1967, its programs were supporting annually about $12 billion in private and public investments in housing and urban development.

This help, for many people in many places, had been a long time coming.

## FIRST MOVES: 1892–1918

The U.S. Congress made its first recorded move in connection with blighted housing on July 20, 1892, when a resolution was passed to provide a special sum of $20,000 for the Secretary of Labor to investigate slums in cities of over 200,000 population. Eventually, a report was prepared disclosing bad housing conditions in four large cities and pinpointing a correlation between the large number of saloons and slum buildings in the decaying areas.

World War I brought with it recognition of the need for some federal action in the housing field. In 1918, the U.S. Shipping Board Emergency Fleet Corporation was authorized to provide housing for people employed in the rapidly expanded shipyards. Loans were provided to real estate firms incorporated under the shipbuilding companies, and the result was construction of 9,000 houses, 1,100 apartment units, 19 dormitories, and 8 hotels in 24 locations where wartime conditions created a shortage of residential dwellings. In effect, this was "company-town" housing. In May and June of that same year, Congress authorized the Bureau of Industrial Housing and Transportation, in the Department of Labor, to work with the U.S. Housing Corporation, created by Presidential executive order, to house war workers. Twenty-five community projects were built to accommodate more than 5,000 families. When the war ended, most of these housing units were sold to private owners, but a few were transferred to other government agencies.

## LEGISLATION DURING THE DEPRESSION

In the early 1930's, individual home ownership and mortgage financing were among the hardest hit victims in a generally sick economy. President Herbert C. Hoover was the first chief executive to focus dramatic attention on housing conditions, relating the state of housing to the general welfare of the nation. Addressing a conference he had called on home building and home ownership in 1931, he said:

> I am confident that the sentiment for home ownership is so embedded in the American heart that millions of people who dwell in tenements, apartments, and rented rows of solid brick have the aspiration for wide opportunity in ownership of their own homes. . . . There can be no fear for a democracy or self-government or for liberty or freedom from home owners, no matter how humble they may be.

In that same speech, President Hoover also noted that the nation had not yet learned how to use its credit structure well enough to encourage young married couples to buy their own homes. And he pointed out that only 46 per cent of all Americans then lived in homes they owned. (Now, that percentage has increased to 62 per cent of a vastly expanded supply of housing, most of which has been built in cities or in towns adjacent to cities.)

### Home Loan Legislation

Before Hoover left office, the Congress enacted the Federal Home Loan Bank Act of 1932 on the recommendation of the housing conference called by the President. The Federal Home Loan Bank Board was authorized to make advances to member home-financing institutions on the basis of first mortgages. More than one million home loans for distressed owners were refinanced from 1933 to 1936.

Although since amended, that FHLB law is still the basic legislation for the Home Loan Bank System of 11 regional institutions that provide financial liquidity and support for 3,973 member home-financing institutions, which can count assets of nearly $18 billion. (Today, savings and loan associations represent the majority of the membership of the Home Loan Bank System, and hold more than 93 per cent of the assets. These institutions, often referred to as "building-and-loans," are designed principally to make loans to home builders and buyers.)

In 1933, the Congress passed the Home Owners' Loan Act to refinance the mortgages of distressed home buyers. An important aspect of this legislation in those confidence-shaken times, when home foreclosures were averaging about 1,000 a day, was a stipulation to authorize the chartering of federal savings and loan associations and the broadening of activities of Federal Home Loan Bank members. A nationwide system for servicing loans and mortgages resulted, with personnel assigned to 458 local, state, and regional offices.

## The National Housing Act of 1934

During his first year in office, President Franklin D. Roosevelt appointed a four-man committee to coordinate government housing activities and to propose federal action to stimulate the residential construction industry.

Members of that committee included Frank C. Walker, Chairman; John H. Fahey, W. Averell Harriman, and Henry I. Harriman. They utilized the services of Winfield W. Riefler, who had been assistant director of research and statistics of the Federal Reserve Board.

Many sources credit Riefler with originating the idea of a government mortgage insurance program. A big mistake of the 1920's had been to build too much housing in the higher price ranges and too little in middle and lower ranges. Also, even in normal times, there was an uncertain supply of mortgage money, and mortgage loans were usually made by local money suppliers who preferred to invest near home. Some lenders were restricted by law to certain areas. First mortgage loans were usually 40 or 50 per cent of appraised value with repayment in from 3 to 15 years at interest rates ranging from 5 to 9 per cent. Obviously, this system encouraged second and even third mortgages at higher rates. Belatedly, lenders learned that a 40 per cent loan on an inflated valuation was a far from sound investment. Riefler came up with his idea for government insurance, and it was presented at the housing committee's first meeting. His proposal seemed a possible solution to the problem of stimulating home building and improvement with the least possible governmental interference in private enterprise.

While the housing committee was discussing Riefler's ideas with the Cabinet, legislation was drafted. Out of the discussions and the legislative conferences came the National Housing Act of 1934, which provided insurance against loss on property-improvement loans, mutual mortgage insurance on homes, and low-cost housing loans up to 80 per cent of appraisal value with up to 20 years for amortization.

That federal housing legislation produced far-reaching results. Delinquent borrowers were given monthly payment (installment-style) loans at liberal rates of interest and the opportunity to save their homes. This scheme, combined with smaller down payments and government insurance of loans, provided the basis of monthly home loan amortization for the Federal Housing Administration (FHA) and, later, the conventional (nongovernment) home loan market.

In passing, it is interesting to note that the National Association of Real Estate Boards (NAREB) endorsed the idea for the crucial Housing Act of 1934 and even contributed to some of the executive level conferences that preceded the drafting of the law. Hugh Potter, then president of NAREB, said: "Establishment by the Federal Government of standards for mortgages eligible for insurance should set up a standard for all home mortgages."*

From the time of its establishment until 1954, the Home Owners' Loan Corporation (HOLC), first set up under the Home Owners' Loan Act, invested nearly $3.5 billion in loans and financial aid to borrowers. Many distressed loans were shored up, as were the financial institutions holding delinquent mortgages. In addition, the HOLC disbursed $490 million to cities and towns to pay for the delinquent taxes of borrowers, as well as the taxes due on properties acquired under foreclosure procedures. All of these actions reinforced the sagging values of residential real estate.

The National Housing Act of 1934 set up the highly important Federal Housing Administration, the Federal National Mortgage Association (now a key marketing factor in the home financing field), and also the stabilizing Federal Savings and Loan Insurance Corporation.

The creation of FHA in the Depression era was the first major move of the federal government to establish a housing program designed to insure long-term mortgage home loans made by private lending institutions—and, just as important, to insure lenders against loss on loans for financing alterations, repairs, and home improvements.†

These federal programs were the beginning of a national trend toward home ownership instead of home rental. From having a minority of families in homes of their own, the nation moved toward its present situation in which a growing majority of American families live in homes to which they hold title—even though that title may be heavily mortgaged. Over

---

* Later, NAREB, whose membership includes more than 80,000 American real estate executives, also approved the setting up of the Federal National Mortgage Association (FNMA), but it withheld approval of early public housing moves and has continued that stand through the years.

† In 1934, the National Bureau of Standards (established in 1901) extended its services for other federal agencies to include those in the housing field, when it began testing of structural materials, investigation of fire-resisting properties of building materials, the study of clay products, and metallurgical research related to residential construction.

the years, Congress amended the National Housing Act to improve conditions for borrowers, liberalizing the insurance of mortgages on new homes for families of moderate income and also providing insurance of mortgages on rental housing projects built by private enterprise.

## New Deal Experiments in Public Housing

During the early Franklin D. Roosevelt years, the federal government included low-cost housing in the National Industrial Recovery Act. As a result, 21,769 public housing units were built—despite legal snarls and public indifference.

In 1935, several "greenbelt" garden towns were laid out by the Resettlement Administration, headed by Rexford G. Tugwell. One of these new garden towns, built with government money on a large tract northeast of Washington, D.C., became known as Greenbelt, Maryland. It pioneered the use of small houses clustered together to leave large green areas for the use of residents. Originally, Greenbelt attracted many government workers, even though they had been unaccustomed to commuting 10 to 15 miles to their jobs. Later, private developments were built up around the new town, and, eventually, the U.S. Government sold the Greenbelt homes to the tenants or anyone who wanted to live in the experimental village—which, today, is still regarded as an attractive place to live.

In his Second Inaugural Address, President Roosevelt spoke eloquently of "one-third of the nation ill-housed." But credit for the passage of the New Deal's major piece of public housing legislation has generally been attributed to the late Democratic Senator from New York, Robert F. Wagner, who had the support of city-minded groups and social reformers. On the whole, Congress regarded the legislation more in the light of an economic stimulant than social reform, but the crucial slum clearance section of the bill stipulated, in an "equivalent elimination" clause, that one unit of slum housing be razed for each new unit of public housing. Eventually, this Act provided funds for 117,755 units of public housing for local housing authorities.

(Under the Truman Administration's Housing Act of 1949, which granted city planners greater flexibility in urban redevelopment, new urban renewal projects automatically eliminated substandard housing. However, that flexibility proviso, in turn, resulted in criticism of the tendency of such projects to destroy substandard housing and then permit construction of luxury and semi-luxury housing beyond the economic reach of former residents of the area—a result that has been particularly evident in the dramatic reconversion of the 500-acre "Southwest" of Washington within a few blocks of the Capitol.)

## EFFECTS OF WORLD WAR II

Even before World War II, the numerous agencies concerned with housing had been reorganized by the federal government. In 1939, the Federal Loan Agency and the Federal Works Agency were set up to coordinate numerous other federal agencies charged with housing functions. Another significant move was made that same year when the Seventy-sixth Congress authorized the Bureau of the Census to obtain data on the characteristics of the nation's housing supply and occupancy in the 1940 census. (This pioneering attempt to find out more about the living conditions of the population has been followed up in subsequent national censuses, and the information has proved beneficial to federal legislative efforts and to the private segment of the residential construction industry.)

But new efforts to coordinate housing programs and the progress of almost all existing federal housing programs were interrupted or modified during World War II, when temporary housing of war workers became a primary consideration. In a sense, this turn of events served to awaken perceptive leaders to the disturbingly low state of the country's residential housing inventory, which became particularly apparent as a large labor force moved from farms and small towns into already crowded industrial centers of population.

Thus, the World War II period in the nation's housing history saw a marked shift from Depression-induced legislation to legislation spurred by the national defense effort. The Lanham Act, in 1940, led to the construction of 945,000 public housing units to accommodate industrial workers who needed shelter while turning out the ships and munitions and equipment for the fighting men on two far-flung fronts.

In 1941, the Seventy-seventh Congress enacted a defense housing amendment, providing liberal mortgage insurance clauses to encourage builders to construct new homes in critical defense areas—an amendment that resulted in 962,000 dwellings for war workers. Later, war veterans were given preference in the allocation of this housing.

## The National Housing Agency

After Pearl Harbor, with the nation's full commitment to the war effort, a new phase of integrating all housing efforts into an essentially single program began. The President established the National Housing Agency, giving it full responsibility for all nonfarm housing programs. Only military base housing was excepted. This action brought the Federal Home Loan Bank, Federal Housing Administration, Public Housing Administration, and Federal National Mortgage Association under one jurisdiction. (In effect, the grouping was the basis for the later formation of the Housing and Home Finance Agency operating complex—destined finally to mature into the Department of Housing and Urban Development with Cabinet status.) The Emergency Price Control Act of 1942 authorized rent controls to help stave off war-induced inflation.

As the war drew to an end, Congress, in 1944, passed the Servicemen's Readjustment Act to authorize guaranty and insurance of GI loans for veterans to purchase, build, or improve homes. A law followed to authorize the use of wartime housing for distressed families of servicemen and veterans and their families and the construction of temporary housing for that purpose. By Executive Order early in 1946, the President named a federal housing expediter to stimulate development. Then, in a move that strengthened the earlier powers granted by the President, the Seventy-ninth Congress passed the Veterans Emergency Housing Act, which established the Office of the Housing Expediter. The Office was empowered to set ceiling prices and rents for new housing and to determine or assign priorities for the delivery of materials or facilities for housing.

In 1947, the new Housing and Rent Act was passed, replacing the Veterans Emergency Housing Act but extending certain of its provisions. At the same time, FHA mortgage insurance was extended, and loans were authorized to finance the manufacture of prefabricated homes, still in the development stage. Subsequently, Reorganization Plan No. 3 set up the Housing and Home Finance Agency to succeed the National Housing Agency and to coordinate and supervise functions of the Home Loan Bank Board, the Federal Housing Administration, and the Public Housing Administration. Also, to help the many new families seeking a place to begin or resume a life interrupted by the war, the National Housing Council was created to bring together representatives of other agencies concerned with housing to abet effective use of federal housing activities.

A year later, comprehensive housing legislation designed to achieve production of up to 1.5 million dwellings a year and to establish a firm national housing policy was proposed. Particularly encouraged were production of lower-cost homes and moderate rental housing, federal aid for slum clearance, and the broadening of a secondary market within government for both FHA- and VA-insured loans—the major activity of FNMA. At this point, the national housing picture had changed, moving out of a wartime perspective.

POSTWAR EXPANSION

Although prewar housing programs were resumed after 1945 on a larger scale, and reinforced by continued or modified war-born federal programs, they were insufficient by themselves to deal with the far-reaching changes and growth of urban communities in the postwar economy. Growing population and rapid urbanization were changing the complexion of the nation, in smaller towns as in large cities. With the shift from a rural to a predominantly urban society had come an increased amount of substandard housing and uncontrolled urban sprawl.

Limited response to the problems of urban expansion came in 1947 with the creation of the Housing and Home Finance Agency. Shortly thereafter, the Housing Act of 1948 aimed to stimulate production of private housing in lower price and rent categories.

The 1948 Act authorized 95 per cent mortgages on thirty-year maturity payment for low-cost homes and 90 per cent mortgages with forty years to repay on low-cost and cooperative projects. Other amendments of this relatively catch-all law dealt with provisions to increase housing for families of limited income. But, during the Eightieth Congress, the much broader Wagner-Ellender-Taft housing bill was shelved, and President Harry S. Truman made housing one of the major themes of his underdog, but successful, campaign for election, repeatedly dubbing the Eightieth as the "do-nothing Congress."

*Housing Act of 1949*

With the surprising Truman election victory came a new Congress, which passed the truly important Housing Act of 1949. This Act added new prestige to the Housing and Home Finance Agency by authorizing broader public housing activity. It also initiated slum clearance and urban redevelopment on a federal basis, and large-scale research into housing and urban problems.

Title I of this Act authorized $1 billion in loans and $500 million in capital grants over a five-year period to localities, as well as advances of funds to assist slum clearance and community development and redevelopment programs. Research studies were set up to find ways of reducing construction and maintenance costs and, also, to increase the production of new housing units. Specifically, too, the Act enabled the District of Columbia to participate in both slum clearance and urban redevelopment. Thus, Washington's already mentioned South-west urban renewal effort was born, although actual razing and rebuilding did not get under way until some years later. In retrospect, many of these basic programs can be seen as the embryonic heart of HUD.

## Racial Covenants Declared Illegal

A milestone in housing history occurred in 1948 when the Supreme Court of the United States held restrictive covenants on private property to be unenforceable as law and contrary to public policy (*Shelley* v. *Kraemer*). As a result, late in 1949, the FHA and other government agencies set up rules to make property with a restrictive racial covenant ineligible for mortgage insurance backed by the government. This was the beginning of a federal fight against segregated housing, to be followed by other government orders designed to encourage the desegregation of residential housing.

## Housing Act of 1950

To encourage greater production of housing for middle-income families, the Housing Act of 1950 was passed. It also authorized FHA insurance of mortgages on low-cost homes in outlying areas, mortgage insurance on cooperative housing projects, and HHFA loans to colleges for student and faculty housing—a major broadening of federal concern for both education and shelter.

## THE EISENHOWER ERA

In 1953, the President's Advisory Committee on Govern-ment Housing Policies and Programs presented a report of considerable consequence. It favored federal assistance to communities to help them eradicate slums, supported the use of long-term FHA mortgage insurance for designated older areas, and urged public and private officials to provide needed housing for minority families. On the basis of the committee's report, President Dwight D. Eisenhower, in a special message to the Eighty-third Congress in 1954, recommended the broadening of existing housing programs to prevent blight and to aid the rehabilitation of salvageable areas. He urged the adoption of a new program of FHA mortgage insurance for housing for low-income families, who might be displaced by slum clearance and similar activities, and the reorganization of FNMA, with the purchase of initial stock by the government and the introduction of private capital funds supplied by users of FNMA.

The Eighty-third Congress passed the Housing Act of 1954, requiring that a community have a workable program for prevention and elimination of slums and blight as a prerequisite for federal assistance to slum clearance and urban renewal; liberalizing FHA mortgage insurance programs to provide more assistance for new housing and the repair or purchase of existing homes; providing a new mortgage insurance program for housing for servicemen; and establishing new protections against abuse of FHA loan insurance programs. (The latter provision was included because investigations had uncovered abuses of the property improvement and postwar rental housing programs, in which some promoters had made unduly large profits on small capital investments, thereby weakening FHA morale and undermining public confidence in federal housing programs.)

In 1955, the Eighty-fourth Congress increased from ten to twenty years the maximum term of residential real estate loans made by national banks and also increased from six to nine months the maximum term for construction loans for financing residential and farm buildings. The Eighty-fourth Congress also increased the extended FHA loan insurance authorization, authorized FHA insurance of mortgages for trailer courts (which have become part of the nation's permanent, rather than mobile, low-price housing), and as part of the Housing Act of 1956, liberalized FHA Title I home repair and improvement loan insurance programs, and FHA mortgages on existing homes and on disaster housing. An entirely new feature was a program of federal assistance for the housing of the elderly through FHA mortgage insurance and low-rent public housing. The 1956 Act also provided for relocation payments to individuals, families, and business displaced by urban renewal.

In 1957, Congress again responded to a Presidential message, with another Housing Act, providing for lower down payments on houses financed with FHA-insured mortgages and liberalizing FHA mortgage insurance programs assisting housing for the elderly. Also, by the terms of the 1957 Act, an individual community could contract for urban renewal grants on a three-quarter federal and one-quarter local basis, if the community picked up the cost of planning, survey, legal work, and administration.

In 1958, the Eighty-fifth Congress acted to stimulate residential construction by reducing down payments on FHA Section 203 houses for sale to individual families and increasing the FNMA special assistance fund by $500 million.

Toward the end of this period, just before the election of President John F. Kennedy, a legislative proposal with HHFA backing and support, for the creation of a department to be concerned with both housing and metropolitan problems was reported favorably by the Senate Banking and Currency Committee, but failed to get voting attention on the Senate floor.

## DEVELOPMENTS IN THE KENNEDY ADMINISTRATION

In February, 1961, President Kennedy directed HHFA Administrator Robert C. Weaver and the Secretary of Commerce to increase their joint planning activities to improve coordination on urban renewal and freeway construction plans in the same areas. The President's 1961 Housing Message listed national objectives as the renewal of cities to assure sound growth, decent living conditions for all Americans, and encouragement of the construction industry.

In 1962, both the Senate and the House turned down President Kennedy's reorganization plan embodying the creation of a department for urban affairs and housing. Defeat in the Senate came first. But, later that year, the Eighty-seventh Congress increased authorization for direct loans by HHFA for rental housing and related facilities for housing of the elderly, thus broadening recognition of the national need for attention to the housing requirements of older citizens. And, although the Eighty-seventh Congress declined to act on the President's request for the new department, it did provide money for loans and grants for public facilities in redevelopment areas where unemployment was a problem. Also, the Housing Act of 1961 authorized new housing programs for low and moderate income families and included in this program the controversial below-market interest rate on FHA-insured rental housing programs. (See Chapter II for more detailed treatment of legislative haggling during the Kennedy period.)

After what many had thought to be a long wait from his first indicated interest during the campaign and his early days in the White House, President Kennedy issued Executive Order 11063 on November 20, 1962, to direct all federal departments and agencies to take action to prevent discrimination in the sale, lease, or occupancy of residential property owned or operated by the federal government. Of course, all programs receiving federal aid were affected by the order. Federal assistance projects were included. However, sanctions on enforcement were applicable only to FHA insurance issued after the effective order.

Many of the nation's largest private builders and some major real estate interests expressed dissatisfaction with the Executive Order. It also found critics among civil rights workers, who thought the action was inadequate and should have been extended to all housing—not just that involved with government support.

Meanwhile, nearly half of the states throughout the land, and many local municipalities, had passed their own fair housing laws and ordinances. In many instances, other projected actions were stalled by reluctant legislators who construed certain segments of public opinion to be the basis for their stand against open housing. (The powerful National

Association of Real Estate Boards took a stand against what it termed "forced housing," but insisted that it was for housing opportunity with freedom of choice for both buyer and seller to sell or buy as they pleased.)

During the early 1960's, there was growing concern over preservation of open space, families displaced by slum clearance, and the first tentative programs to assist the development of urban mass transit. (The Mass Transportation Act of 1964 authorized HHFA to make loans and grants for facilities and equipment, and some solid appropriations were made to implement the program.)

New programs, introduced prior to the enactment of HUD legislation, included a low-interest-rate loan for rehabilitation in urban renewal areas, mortgage insurance for nonprofit nursing homes, and a new type of urban renewal to emphasize code enforcement in bringing blighted housing up to a decent living standard.

States, counties, and municipalities were showing more and more interest in participating in these and other federally sponsored programs. In large part, their interest was based on the availability of U.S. funds on a matching basis, with the state and local share being smaller than the federal contribution, and there was scant enthusiasm for any new state or local housing legislation that did not include provisions for some federal subsidy.

## The Situation in 1965

Just before HUD came into being as a Cabinet department, the numerical record for the complex of federal housing agencies that had gone before showed these accomplishments over the years:

Total FHA mortgage insurance in excess of $105 billion, with assistance to home ownership or improvement in living conditions extended to more than 37 million families;

More than 2 million Americans living in public housing projects with an improved standard of living;

More than 790 communities actively participating in urban

renewal programs involving nearly 1,700 projects approved in land areas of 124 square miles—the equivalent of 3 major cities;

Some 400 open space grants worth about $46 million and covering 147,000 acres;

Urban assistance planning grants in the amount of $100 million covering 2,286 projects;

Commitments totaling about 160,000 units for housing older citizens;

More than 2,500 college housing loans in the amount of nearly $3 billion to accommodate more than 646,000 students in colleges and teaching hospitals, with about one-third of all students in institution-owned college housing throughout the country living in facilities assisted by the college housing program;

Mass transit grants of more than $110 million made to help communities and areas solve their problems;

A total of 41 low-income housing demonstration grants costing $6.7 million.

That was where HUD was to find it stood statistically when it took inventory of the work of its predecessor agencies. Despite their accomplishments, the Department into which they were melded faced a difficult future. Wherever Americans lived, there were problems that, as President Johnson reminded Congress and the country in March, 1965, were "already in the front rank of national concern and interest." And, the President said, "they deserve to be in the front rank of government as well."

# II

# How HUD Happened

When the Department of Housing and Urban Development was signed into law (P.L. 89–174) on Thursday, September 9, 1965, the United States was ready to accept its eleventh executive department. The action became effective sixty days later, although President Johnson could have made it operable earlier by Executive Order.

The legislative creation of HUD followed a five-year effort spanning both the Kennedy and Johnson administrations. Prior to that period, as summarized in Chapter I, there had been three decades of federal interest and legislation, during which private housing mortgages had been stabilized, rental housing built for poor families, and urban renewal and other special programs created to assist in setting up broad community facilities in many localities.

Final passage of the HUD law reflected the efforts of supporting members of the House and Senate and their staff and committee aides on Capitol Hill; the effectiveness of legislative proposals offered and revised over the years by the staff of the general counsel of the Housing and Home Finance Agency and the Agency's increasingly effective liaison with legislators on the Hill; and the accruing support of important segments of the housing industry, the U.S. Conference of Mayors, and other groups. Generally, opposition sprang from a majority of Republicans and Southern Democrats in both the House and Senate.

Many of the arguments for establishing a Cabinet department were based on the need for managerial improvement and greater efficiency and coordination of programs, but there was, also, general recognition that the prestige of Cabinet status would benefit housing and urban programs both in Congress and outside government.

Added prestige was an element of particular significance for the 13,600 scattered employees concerned in the effort to bring together all the existing programs. Interestingly, and not unnaturally, although key personnel agreed that an added degree of prestige was essential to successful expansion of housing and urban programs within the federal establishment, the fight to achieve Cabinet status had also to overcome the built-in reluctance of some officials who regarded the creation of a new department as having a diminishing effect on their established power bases.

It is important to note that Robert C. Weaver, as administrator of the HHFA, had little actual authority over other federal housing components—FHA, FNMA, and various public housing, urban renewal, and community facilities programs. The HHFA administrator enjoyed a position of leadership, but that position did not carry with it essential influence over the programs of other agencies, particularly those responsible for urban renewal and public housing programs.

Before the creation of HUD, the federal housing hierarchy included under the HHFA office five operating units: the FHA, Public Housing Administration, and FNMA—each specifically authorized by law—and the Community Facilities Administration and Urban Renewal Administration, created within the HHFA framework but without specific Congressional authorization.

Particularly at issue during the hearings on the creation of HUD was the status of FHA, whose existence was zealously guarded by private housing groups, such as the National Association of Real Estate Boards, and the Mortgage Bankers Association. Although the original House version of the bill would have transferred the functions of FHA to HUD and provided an assistant secretary to administer programs for the private mortgage money market, the final legislation retained FHA as a separate entity in HUD under the federal housing commissioner, who was designated as an assistant HUD secretary.

## BACKGROUND OF PROPOSALS FOR A DEPARTMENT

Long before housing and urban problems were formally recognized by Congress, Washington had heard proposals for a Cabinet-level department to help cities and small communities whose needs in renewing public facilities and in grappling with slums and blight had outstripped revenues. A "Department of Municipalities," which would have functioned only as a study group, was suggested even before World War I. Years later, in 1934, Charles E. Merriam of the National Resources Board called for a voice for the cities and, by 1942, he was urging a separate administrative agency in Washington to care for the interests of cities. In 1954, a specific proposal for establishment of a "Department of Urbiculture" was introduced in Congress by Representative J. Arthur Younger, Republican of California. A number of similar bills continued to be introduced, and during the second Eisenhower term, when Albert M. Cole was head of HHFA, a housing department bill, sponsored by Senate Democrats, received favorable comment from the Bureau of the Budget, which noted that the proposal was a move in the right direction. Reported favorably by the Senate Banking and Currency Committee, the bill was not tested by a vote in either legislative branch. Nonetheless, that much progress in a Republican administration was regarded as significant.

Thus, there was not much surprise over the 1960 Democratic platform endorsement of Cabinet rank for housing and urban development. Nor was it unexpected that President Kennedy warned, in his State of the Union Message of January 30, 1961: "Our cities are being engulfed in squalor. Twelve long years after Congress declared our goal to be a decent home and suitable environment for every American family, we still have 25 million Americans living in sub-standard homes."

## THE JOCKEYING UNDER JFK

In spite of a climate that had appeared increasingly to favor the idea of a department, when the first Kennedy Administration–backed bill was reported out of committee in both the House and Senate, it was regarded as in jeopardy. A preliminary voting head count in the Senate had shown strong Southern Democratic and Republican opposition. Nevertheless, Administration forces decided to risk a vote, but the House Rules Committee delayed action and the issue was not joined.

In 1962, the House Rules Committee again considered the proposal, but on January 24, by a nine-to-six vote, refused to approve it for floor action, thus killing the bill.

At that time, opposition had been mounted by the National Association of Home Builders (See Chapter VIII), which feared a downgrading of emphasis on private home construction. The National Association of Real Estate Boards had expressed worry that the FHA status would be lessened. Southern Democrats and other conservative interests had also voiced opposition, with the House Republican Policy Committee going on record as opposed.

After the unfavorable House Rules Committee vote, President Kennedy was reported disturbed. He had not mentioned a housing order in his second State of the Union message, apparently in an effort to placate the opposition. But, on the evening of January 24, he said, at a press conference, that he was "rather astonished" at the unfavorable vote and would introduce a reorganization plan to accomplish his housing department ambition. In answer to what is generally acknowledged to have been a planted question at the press meeting, the President also said that he would name Robert C. Weaver as head of the proposed department if it were established. This move was interpreted as an attempt to put Republicans on the defensive on both the housing and race issues involved in the possible appointment of Weaver, a Negro. However, by the time the Reorganization Plan, which would have become effective within 60 days unless either House rejected it by a majority vote, was submitted to Congress on January 30, 1962, Republicans were less on the defensive than on the warpath.

When Kennedy served notice that he would make an all-out effort to establish the new department through the vehicle of a reorganization plan (used successfully by Eisenhower in giving the Federal Security Agency Cabinet-level status as the new Department of Health, Education, and Welfare, in 1953), he was announcing his intent to bypass the Rules Committee, which had recorded all five Committee Republicans and four of its ten Democrats against the bill. The effect of the President's statement was to enlarge the importance of the urban affairs proposal as a political issue. *The Washington Post,* on January 25, 1962, reported:

> It looked as though this [political motive] were the reason for pushing for a Rules Committee vote yesterday. Democratic leaders knew they were licked in the committee, but they asked for a vote before the President's televised press conference, apparently in hopes of spotlighting Republic opposition to helping cities.

Four Southern Democrats voted against the plan, Chairman Howard W. Smith, of Virginia, Representatives William M. Colmer, of Mississippi, Carl Elliott, of Alabama, and James W. Trimble, of Arkansas. The last two were normally Administration supporters, but both faced re-election problems in their rural Southern districts. President Kennedy's statement, made, as noted, during a press conference immediately after the Rules Committee rebuff, that he would appoint Weaver to head the proposed new Cabinet department, did not help their situation. Kennedy then said that he

> had gotten the impression two weeks ago, after reading reports of the meeting in Oklahoma, that they [the Republicans] shared

our concern for more effective management and responsibility of the problems of two-thirds of our population which lived in cities.

But he added:

> The Urban Affairs Department proposal has been plagued by two principal lines of opposition. One comes from the rural conservative Congressmen who see it as the beginning of a big spending program with nothing in it for them. The other, not talked about openly, is the civil rights opposition of Southerners to a bill that would pave the way for the first Negro cabinet member.

Of course, these remarks served to bring both issues to the surface, but with a reverse twist. One day later, Wisconsin's John W. Byrnes, Chairman of the House Republican Policy Committee, denounced the President's "callous attempt" to use the race issue to win Congressional approval for his proposal. Highlighting his remarks, Byrnes placed in the *Congressional Record* an exchange of telegrams with Eugene Reed, the New York State President of the NAACP. Reed, in his telegram, warned Byrnes that Republican opposition to the creation of the new department "will be interpreted as Republican opposition to a possible Negro Cabinet appointment." In reply, Byrnes argued that the GOP Policy Committee actually opposed the new department "as a dangerous attempt to centralize more power in the Federal Government at the expense of the individual states."

Chalmers M. Roberts summarized the plight of the Republicans at this juncture in *The Washington Post,* January 26, 1962:

> The Republicans have been wailing about their losses in the big cities, where the Negro vote is concentrated. If they reject Weaver, and that is the way the vote will be described next fall, they can expect an outpouring of Democratic votes that will punch big holes in GOP hopes of capturing the House, their major 1962 objective.

If the Republicans decide they can't risk that and so vote for Weaver, or let the plan become fact without a roll call, the Northern and Western Democrats will surely remind every Negro voter next fall of the high honor done them by Mr. Kennedy.

Roberts also recalled that this state of affairs was especially ironic because in the fall election Republican Vice-Presidential candidate Henry Cabot Lodge had promised that if Richard Nixon were elected he would name a Negro to his Cabinet. Nixon, alarmed about what such a pledge would do to his chances in the South, backed down at the cost of key votes in the Northern states—the area where Kennedy found his slim margin of victory.

The Republican-Conservative argument was voiced again on January 28, 1962, by Senate Minority Leader Everett McK. Dirksen of Illinois. The Associated Press quoted him as asking: "Do we want to set up a department for direct dealings between Washington and the municipalities, which are adjuncts of the states?" He answered his own question by saying he didn't believe this would be wise.

Three days later, on January 31, House GOP leader Charles A. Halleck of Indiana bolstered the Republican attack by calling Kennedy's actions "sham tactics" to cover up Democratic shortcomings in the area of civil rights legislation.

Walter Lippmann gave what amounted to the liberal rebuttal on February 1, in his column:

> Why, it will be asked, is this a good thing to have done from Washington? The answer is that it cannot be done adequately and as a matter of fact is not being done adequately, by the states and municipalities. There are several reasons for that. One reason is that in the state legislatures the urban voters are grossly underrepresented as against the rural voters. Another reason is that the expanding metropolitan areas overlap state and county and municipal lines, and if they are to be governed properly, development must be planned on a metropolitan scale. The planning and development cannot be done merely by the

localities of the past which are now being swallowed up by the metropolis.

Lippmann then theorized over the choice of Weaver for the new Cabinet post:

> . . . he is no doubt the main reason for the opposition of the Southern Democrats. But he cannot be the reason for the opposition of the Republican leaders who are making all sorts of gestures, no doubt sincerely, to prove themselves to be friends of the Negro voters.
>
> I cannot help thinking that the Republicans did not stop to consider what they were doing, and that they acted on their reflexes, which take it for granted that any new proposal to deal with the changing world is automatically undesirable.

Although much Republican opposition sprang from party-line unity, another explanation can be suggested: with one exception, the Republican leaders of the House simply were not urban. Minority leader Halleck came from Rensselaer, Indiana, population 4,470; minority whip Leslie C. Arends, Melvin, Illinois, population 500; House Republican Conference Chairman Charles B. Hoeven, Alton, Iowa, population 1,048; ranking Republican on the House Rules Committee Clarence Brown, who at one time had been editor of a newspaper in Blanchester, Ohio, population 2,944. The sole ranking House Republican from a city of more than 5,000 was Byrnes, from Green Bay, Wisconsin, population 62,888. Nor were the Republicans alone in this orientation: Howard Smith, Chairman of the House Rules Committee came from the tiny hamlet of Broad Run, Virginia, and the number two man on the same committee, Colmer, was from Pascagoula, Mississippi, population 17,155.

The Republicans' almost solid front against Cabinet status for urban affairs was also based on philosophic disagreement with many of the existing programs involving public housing, urban renewal, and community facilities. They seemed to feel that official federal extension of influence in the revamping

and rehabilitation of cities would mean increased expenditures
—and also control of the programs by the party in power, the
Democrats.

The Republican opposition also included a number of legislators who had been known to be friendly to existing FHA and
FNMA mortgage programs and were determined to have them
continue as operating entities. They apparently feared that the
value of those existing government housing programs might
be weakened if they were included in the same department
that would administer community planning and (according
to the plans of the day) transportation. In addition, some observers of the Washington legislative scene noted, the Kennedy
proposals for urban affairs did not have the powerful, White
House–based legislative liaison that is always required to obtain favorable attention for an important new law.

Seeking to establish a record for future election leverage,
and also harboring some hope of having the reorganization
plan approved, the Administration recognized that quick
Senate approval was required to influence the more conservative House. In an effort to speed up the vote, Senator Gale
McGee, a supporter of the plan, introduced a resolution to
reject it, and the resolution went to the Senate Government
Operations Committee. Two weeks of bizarre, supercharged
maneuvering followed. Senator John McClellan, Democrat of
Arkansas, held leisurely hearings, prompting the Administration to recognize that Senate delay would enable the House to
act first. Thereupon the President obtained an informal agreement with the minority leadership in the House to wait for the
Senate vote. But the bulk of Republican representatives would
not follow the leadership and pressed for a vote.

At that point, the Senate maneuvered to get a prior vote by
using a discharge motion to prevent the chairman and committee, who were favorable to the plan but unfavorable to the
discharge resolution, from forestalling a floor vote on the
resolution. Since debate is limited strictly on a discharge motion, Administration supporters asked an opponent of the plan

to introduce a motion to discharge the committee in order to get the Senate vote set up ahead of the scheduled House vote.

However, the discharge motion set off a bitter debate and put Administration supporters on the defensive. Chairman McClellan protested the motion as an "affront" to the Senate committee system. Other moderate senators, who favored creation of a department, were unhappy with the procedure and tactics used to speed up the Senate vote because they interpreted the strategy as belittling to both the committee and the entire Senate. The discharge motion was defeated by a 58-to-42 vote, with 38 Democrats and 4 Republicans being overcome by a combination of 26 Democrats and 32 Republicans who fought the discharge motion maneuver. Next day, the House, voting first, rejected the reorganization plan, 264 to 150, with a combination of 111 Democrats and 153 Republicans holding the power over 137 Democrats and only 13 Republicans.

The vote might have been closer, but still unsuccessful, had the Senate approved the plan or at least not used the discharge ploy unsuccessfully. Obviously, the procedural issue involved cost the proposal crucial votes in the Senate in 1962. Of the senators who helped to defeat the discharge motion in 1962, fourteen switched their votes three years later to support the successful HUD legislative action. Most of them would probably have voted for a department the first time, had it not been for their deep feeling in the matter of procedure.

After the 1962 defeat of the reorganization proposal, President Kennedy issued his long-awaited Executive Order barring discrimination in government-backed housing. Then, in 1963, he again urged the establishment of the new department in his Budget Message, but made no meaningful attempt to follow up.

### The LBJ Drive

President Lyndon B. Johnson first recommended establishment of a department in his Housing and Community Development Message in 1964, but no Administration bill was put in motion. The full drive was reserved for 1965, after the

Democratic sweep of 1964 put seventy-one new Democrats in House seats.

It was in his Budget Message in late January, 1965, that President Johnson again called for the establishment of a department for housing and urban development. He repeated his plea in his Message on the Cities on March 2, 1965, when he pointed out:

> This new Department will provide a focal point for thought and innovation and imagination about the problems of our cities . . . it will work to strengthen the constructive relationships between nation, state and city—the creative federalism—which is essential to progress. This partnership will demand the leadership of mayors, Governors and state legislatures . . .
>
> We have over nine million homes, most of them in cities, which are run down or deteriorating; over four million do not have running water or even plumbing. Many of our central cities are in need of major surgery to overcome decay. New suburban sprawl reaches out into the countryside, as the process of urbanization consumes a million acres a year. The old, the poor, the discriminated against are increasingly concentrated in central city ghettos, while others move to the suburbs, leaving the central city to battle against immense odds.
>
> Physical decay, from obsolescent schools to polluted water and air, helps breed social decay. It casts a pall of ugliness and despair on the spirits of the people. And this is reflected in rising crime rates, school dropouts, delinquency and social disorganization.

At the behest of the Administration, a draft bill was introduced in the House on March 23 by Wisconsin Representative Henry S. Reuss, and seven days later Representative Dante B. Fascell, of Florida, submitted an identical bill—the one to be considered in the House. On the Senate side, Abraham A. Ribicoff, of Connecticut, introduced draft legislation, on March 25, that conformed essentially to proposals made by the Administration in the Eighty-seventh and in the Eighty-eighth Congresses.

At hearings of the Subcommittee on Executive and Legislative Reorganization of the House Government Operations Committee on April 5 and 6, support was placed on the record by Mayor Richard C. Lee of New Haven, Connecticut, for the U.S. Conference of Mayors, of which he was a past president. Close observers of the HUD formation period have recalled that Mayor Lee was highly effective in working for the idea of a department, displaying an ability to aid the Administration cause by enlisting Congressional support without raising hackles, or thorny issues.

Other supporting groups were the American Municipal Association, the National Association of Housing and Redevelopment Officials, the National League of Cities, the National Association of Counties, the National Housing Conference, the National Association of Home Builders, the American Institute of Planners, the American Institute of Architects, the AFL-CIO, and the National Association of Mutual Savings Banks.

Opposition was generated by the unwavering National Association of Real Estate Boards, the Chamber of Commerce of the United States, the National Association of Manufacturers, and the Mortgage Bankers Association (whose main concern was preservation of the essential FHA functions as an entity).

In representing NAREB, whose opposition has been regarded as the most effective, but influencing relatively few votes, lobbyist John C. Williamson testified that creation of HUD would "at best generate a cold war among the Departments of the Executive Branch as it sought to envelop within its jurisdiction all the programs geared to the needs and aspirations of the urban community."

Both the National Association of County Officials and the National Association of Home Builders switched from earlier opposition in 1961 and 1962 to support the 1965 HUD effort. The NAHB switch was strategic and effective. Obviously, the status and work of NAHB executive Bernard L. Boutin, a former mayor of Laconia, New Hampshire, and a Kennedy appointee to the General Services Administration a few years earlier, were helpful. He put his NAHB group on the record in strong accord with a recommendation that an assistant secretary be designated to handle, under the supervision of the Secretary, programs dealing with the private mortgage market.

The Deputy Director of the Bureau of the Budget, Elmer B. Staats, testified in favor of HUD, pointing out that it would provide authority for more effective direction and coordination of the closely interrelated programs of HHFA.

When the House Committee on Government Operations reported the bill favorably on May 11 by a vote of twenty to eight, an amendment was added to designate that one of the assistant secretaries be charged with the administration, under the Secretary's direction, of the programs relating to the private mortgage money market for housing. The majority view was that the timing was appropriate for the new department that would not take over any agencies or programs not already in HHFA. The minority view, as stated by seven Republicans, included a statement that the bill was "another manifestation of the perennial urge to classify problems as having outstripped the capacity of state and local governments and to create new federal departments to solve them."

With a vote of 217 to 184 on a roll call, the House passed the HUD bill on June 16, a day after a motion to recommit the legislation had been defeated 259 to 141. The recommittal motion, as proposed by Republican Florence P. Dwyer of New Jersey, would have sent the bill back to the Committee on Government Operations with instructions to report back a Republican alternate measure calling for an Office of Urban Affairs and Community Development in the Executive Office of the President.

Undoubtedly, the key consideration in the defeat of the Dwyer motion was that it had the votes of 259 Democrats, many of them Southerners whose support was needed to keep the original bill alive—but who, next day, were permitted to vote against it for the record, which showed 42 fewer votes from Democrats. Also, it has been noted that the 59 votes defeating the recommittal included 254 Democrats and only 5 Republicans, as opposed to 19 Democrats and 122 Republicans, far stronger on Democratic support than the unsuccessful effort in 1962. The change in the House has been interpreted as due about half to the influence of electoral changes and half to switches of votes. A number of reasons have been advanced to explain the switch of 47 Southern Democrats who had opposed Kennedy on a department in 1962, but who saved HUD for Johnson in 1965.

The changes in the structure of the original opposition that had blocked the Kennedy measure once more came to the attention of pundits and public alike. There was general agreement that the Southern Democrats had been blunted in large measure by Weaver's creditable performance on projects in their home areas as administrator of the HHFA and by the overwhelming Johnson victory in the fall elections, and that the conservatives, too, had been caught by the Johnson sweep and the curbing of the power of the House Rules Committee, their bastion, on January 5, 1965. As for the lobbies, *The New York Times* noted that: "cracks in this opposition have appeared." Pivotal among the changes in posture was that of the National Association of Home Builders. (See Chapter VIII.)

President Johnson was so pleased with the House passage of the bill that he called a news conference to note that the tally was "impressive and decisive and exceeded our expectations."

After success in the House, where the essential HUD battle had had to be won, the Senate action was something of an anticlimax—but, nevertheless, meaningful as well as necessary. When the Senate Government Operations Committee's Executive Reorganization Subcommittee held hearings that began March 31 and continued on April 1 and 2, and on May 19, the testimony took some of its tenor from the House. Pennsylvania's Joseph S. Clark continued his long support of the HUD legislative effort by noting that city people need an advocate in Washington to keep up with the farmers, representing only 7 per cent of the population but having a Cabinet department for a century.

Senator Clark also credited his long-time friend, the late Herbert H. Lehman, with having been the originator of the first Senate bill offered to create a "Department of Urban Affairs" in 1955. (The Younger proposal for an "Urbiculture" department had been a year earlier.) Clark said that Lehman was among the first to understand the "need to create for the urban community . . . an agency at the Federal Government level of sufficient dignity to enable it to exist on equal terms at the Cabinet table."

Other supporting testimony came from New York's Mayor Robert F. Wagner who discounted the opposition contention that creation of HUD would sacrifice some states' rights, and local authority and effectiveness. Boston's Mayor John F. Collins warned against delaying HUD for further Congressional consideration of inclusion of more agencies in a new department. Collins stressed the need for action in 1965. And National Housing Conference President Nathaniel S. Keith added support and the thought that the HUD bill would provide the basis for the kind of administration needed to handle new programs that would be legislated later.

Lukewarm opposition—or, from another view, half-hearted support—came from the Mortgage Bankers Association, which was skeptical about the need for a department, but wanted mainly to be assured that FHA would be continued in its separate and independent role, with a commissioner appointed by the President with the approval of the Senate. (An amendment to that effect was urged by MBA president C. C. Cameron.)

A spokesman for the American Farm Bureau Federation

argued against the establishment of a department on the basis that it would handle functions that were "primarily a private and local responsibility."

When the Senate Committee on Government Operations reported the bill favorably on the basis of a nine-to-four vote, its version did not include the House stipulation that the President make a study of functions in other agencies that might be transferred to a department. The committee's negative votes were cast by Chairman McClellan, a Democrat, and Republicans Carl T. Curtis, of Nebraska, Karl E. Mundt, of South Dakota, and Milward L. Simpson, of Wyoming.

The committee adopted several amendments to the draft bill. For instance, Senator Ribicoff's amendment specified that an assistant secretary be designated to administer HUD programs relating to the private mortgage money market. Another, by Senator Robert F. Kennedy, required the President to make a study of functions in other federal agencies that might be transferred to a new department. The committee's approving report noted that the Bureau of the Budget had said the department's functions should, for reasons of clarity involving assimilation of other related government agencies, be limited to those then in HHFA. But the committee noted its desire to see the department obtain jurisdiction of functions dealing with the physical improvement of metropolitan areas.

When the Senate passed the bill by a 57 to 33 roll call vote on August 11, the major difference from the House version was the Senate provision to enable FHA to retain its identity under a commissioner appointed by the President and working under the supervision and direction of the HUD Secretary. Senator John J. Sparkman, Democrat, of Alabama, long regarded as a favorite by private housing interests, proposed the amendment that was accepted by the Senate—despite a provision, already in the House version, that one of the assistant secretaries be given a portfolio to administer programs relating to the private mortgage market.

When the Senate and House bills went to conference, it was

agreed that FHA would retain its separate identity under a commissioner who would be an assistant secretary and that he would also handle, under the HUD Secretary, all other Department programs relating to the private mortgage money market. Earlier, the House had rejected language similar to that adopted by the Senate, but the conference compromise was worked out to give FHA higher status.

The conference agreement also required the HUD Secretary to work with state governors and agencies and to hold informal public hearings on federal and state urban development projects. Language setting up a director of Urban Program Coordination was worked out, as was a provision to require the President to undertake a study of federal functions in other established agencies that might be placed in HUD and to so recommend to the Congress. The Senate's stipulation directing the Secretary to encourage private housing in federal programs and to develop cooperation with private enterprise was made a part of the final compromise HUD legislation that was accepted by the Senate on August 30, and by the House a day later. Both voice votes were taken without debate.

In reviewing the bill's passage in the Senate, observers have noted that 57 votes for the bill in 1965 were contrasted to 42 losing votes in 1962. In 1965, the bill passed with a coupling of 47 Democratic votes in the Senate and 10 Republican, against 4 Democrats and 19 Republicans. The voting 3 years earlier had counted 38 Democrats and 4 Republicans for a Cabinet department against the prevailing combination of 26 Democratic senators and 32 Republican. Some turnaround in the voting was due to electoral changes, but the 14 senators who switched their votes to approval were both essential and sufficient for the difference that meant victory in 1965. Among the 19 Republicans and 14 Democrats who voted against the 1965 bill in the Senate, 12 were from Southern states. Alan Bible of Nevada and Frank J. Lausche of Ohio were the only Northern Democrats to vote against HUD in 1965.

President Johnson signed the HUD bill on September 9. But he failed to name the man who would head the new Department.

Weeks of speculation and conjecture followed in the public prints and in private Washington conversations.

When Johnson allowed the bill to become law in November, 1965, without naming Weaver—who, in effect, as HHFA chief, was functioning as acting head of HUD—to the post, speculation increased that the Secretaryship would go to someone else. The delay brought up names of a number of possible nominees. Reported to have been considered were then Mayor Wagner of New York City, Mayor Lee of New Haven, Connecticut, Whitney Young, then executive director of the Urban League, Mayor Richard J. Daley of Chicago, and Albert Rains, long a liberal friend of housing, who was not seeking re-election to his long-held House seat from an Alabama district.

By the time Weaver won Johnson's nod in mid-January, 1966, the appointment came as something of an anticlimax and generated no opposition of any significance.

Weaver's appointment as Secretary capped a government career that began in 1933. He had worked in the federal housing, defense, and manpower fields until 1944, when he became a race relations expert for the city of Chicago and then a lecturer at Northwestern, Columbia, and New York universities. Later, he had served as deputy commissioner for housing and as rent administrator in New York state, sitting in Governor Harriman's cabinet for three years. In 1960, while he was vice-chairman of the New York City Housing and Redevelopment Board, he was called by President Kennedy to return to Washington as HHFA boss.

His new job as Secretary carried broad responsibilities. Vested in the Office of Secretary of Housing and Urban Development under Public Law 89–174 were all of the functions, powers, and duties of the Housing and Home Finance Agency (including the Community Facilities and Urban Renewal administrations), the Federal Housing Administration, the Federal National Mortgage Association, and the Public Housing Administration, and the numerous offices of all these agencies.

## THE VICTORY IN RETROSPECT

What is the proper perspective on the reasons for the victory in 1965 of the Johnson Administration—a victory denied Kennedy only three years earlier, and a victory that made the quiet appointment of Dr. Weaver possible? A *Washington Post* editorial at the time described the situation:

> The House vote for creation of a Cabinet-level department concerned with housing and urban development may be attributed in part to President Johnson's influence on Capitol Hill. The contrast between the 217–184 vote and the House's rejection of President Kennedy's reorganization order designed to accomplish the same purpose is indeed striking. Three years ago the Kennedy measure went down by a vote of 264–150. It would be naive, however, to suppose that the more favorable climate for this change has come about solely as a result of political influence and maneuvering. We surmise that a larger factor in the outcome was the growing apprehension about the state of urban affairs in the United States. An increasing number of city dwellers are worried about congestion, stalled transportation, slums, crime, urban sprawl, pollution, rising taxes and so forth. The problems of our cities are multiplying even faster than their population, and not much is being done to relieve the mounting burdens.

One worry, carrying over from the earliest proposals to almost the final passage in 1965, concerned a name for the proposed new department. Some fifty different bills and proposals for a department concerned with housing and cities had been made, most of them containing the words "housing," "urban," "cities," "development," or "affairs," but with varying emphasis. It was something of a triumph merely to get a fairly well-accepted name approved. The National Association of Home

Builders had been adamant that "housing" had to come first and foremost. The nation's mayors had been strong for stressing "cities" or "urban." Both were placated in the final selection.

Whatever the new department might have been called, by the time it was established nearly everybody had come to accept some basic premises. In communities of all sizes, municipal revenues had simply proven insufficient to meet the proliferation of urban problems. As a result, there was undeniable need for consolidating federal programs involving grants, loans, and technical assistance to urban areas.

In a summarizing statement on the HUD legislation before the Senate Executive Reorganization Subcommittee, Kermit Gordon, former director of the Bureau of the Budget, noted that the bill set out ". . . as a matter of national purpose the sound development of the nation's urban communities and metropolitan areas in which the vast majority of its people live and work."

# III

# How HUD Is Organized

At the time HUD came into being, Robert Weaver, as head of the Housing and Home Finance Agency, was working closely with FHA Commissioner Philip N. Brownstein, Commissioner Marie C. McGuire of the Public Housing Administration (PHA), and President J. Stanley Baughman of the Federal National Mortgage Association (FNMA). Administrator Weaver was also responsible for the programs of two somewhat independent units within HHFA's own framework: the Community Facilities Administration, then under the direction of Acting Commissioner Richard L. Still, and the Urban Renewal Administration, directed by Commissioner William L. Slayton.

For various reasons, these agencies and units were only loosely controlled by the Office of the HHFA Administrator, although that Office was charged with the responsibility for coordinating their programs. The FHA, PHA, and FNMA had all been established separately and prior to the HHFA. The top officials of FHA and PHA were appointed directly by the President; FNMA was an independent financial structure, almost as much out of government as in it. The commissioners of the units within HHFA itself were appointed by the HHFA administrator after consultation with the President, but drew outside support from their political bases. For instance, Commissioner Slayton's strength and sphere of interest derived from the mayors of big cities and from his own former connections with downtown Washington renewal programs, which had involved widespread razing of buildings and displacement of former residents.

In addition to coordinating the work of all these constituent agencies and units, the Office of the Housing Administrator was also charged with studying national housing needs and preparing recommendations for the President and Congress. Specifically, it was responsible for:

Carrying out a program of urban studies and housing research;

Approving programs developed by local communities to prevent and eliminate slums and certifying federal urban renewal aids as available;

Administering programs of grants and loans to aid urban mass transportation, and transportation research and demonstration grants;

Administration of grants to public or private organizations to carry out demonstrations of new methods of improving low-income housing and housing for the handicapped.

During this period, FHA acted as a separate agency—under the broad HHFA structure, but through its own seventy-six insuring officers and six multifamily housing offices—to insure loans on private homes, multifamily rental and housing projects, cooperative housing, military housing, nursing homes, housing for the aged and handicapped, and, also, loans for property rehabilitation, repair, and improvement. Its other responsibilities included analyses of local housing markets and determination of minimum property standards. The Housing Act of 1965 also enabled the FHA to insure mortgages for purchase of land and to insure home mortgages for all veterans who had not used VA mortgage insurance.

The Public Housing Administration, operating through seven regional offices, handled the federally aided low-rent public housing programs authorized by the Housing Act of 1937, as amended. This program entailed loans, support of loans to local housing authorities to help finance development and construction, and contributions to local authorities to keep rents at levels within reach of low-income tenants. The 1965 Act provided authority for local. housing. authorities to lease or buy and rehabilitate existing housing for low-rent programs.

The Federal National Mortgage Association, through five agency offices and a New York City sales office, used secondary market operations to buy and sell FHA- and VA-insured home mortgages to maintain an effective market.

The Community Facilities Administration handled a number of programs under which it made interest-free advances to communities for the planning of public works and to state and local governments for community facilities and, also, 3 per cent loans to educational institutions to build student and faculty housing and to nonprofit corporations to build rental housing for the elderly and the handicapped. Its seven regional offices operated through seven regional HHFA offices.

The Urban Renewal Administration, through the same regional offices, made loans and grants to localities to plan and carry out slum clearance and urban renewal programs, grants to states and local planning agencies for comprehensive planning, and grants to assist public bodies to demonstrate methods of slum clearance and acquire developed and undeveloped land for preservation as open spaces.

These programs, with their individual objectives, had tended each to develop a singleness of purpose and outlook that prompted observers to regard them as uncoordinated, despite the over-all alliance under the HHFA administrator. He was looked upon as something of a superchief with little real power over the functions of his subsidiary chiefs—the ones who administered the specific programs and allocated the money.

## THE CHANGES UNDER HUD

When HUD was established as a Cabinet department responsible for all existing federal housing and urban programs previously administered by HHFA and its constituent agencies, it was also charged with instituting new programs authorized in the Housing and Urban Development Act of 1965. The most important included rent supplements for lower-income families; additional neighborhood facilities; code enforcement grants; and the lease and purchase of housing for low-income families as a new facet of public housing assistance.

However, when Robert Weaver took over as Secretary, his initial obligation was to bring together the long-standing programs, such as FHA and FNMA, in the new Cabinet hierarchy and there establish a close cooperative relationship between them and the new programs, such as the rent supplements, and those older urban renewal and public housing programs that were felt to have gone somewhat off course.

In his early HHFA years, Secretary Weaver had instituted weekly meetings of his program commissioners. Fully recognizing the status of the FHA and Public Housing commissioners—both Presidential appointees like himself—and the unique quasi-governmental position of FNMA, he had used persuasion and diplomacy to try to coordinate their aims and projects.

Now, he had the authority to set forth broad new organizational patterns. These he outlined to President Johnson in February, 1966:

> I herewith submit the organization plan of the Department of Housing and Urban Development. The plan will become effective over a period of time by the orderly transfer of duties and responsibilities within the Department. The plan has three basic objectives: (1) to redesign the Department so that it can deal efficiently and thoroughly with the problems of urban America; (2) to provide strong decision-making authority in the field, through regional offices; (3) to prepare a sound management framework through which the Demonstration Cities program can be successfully carried out."

As Weaver also pointed out, his plan was designed to meet the five basic goals that the President had set up for the new Department in his January, 1966, Message on the Cities. The President had made it clear that (1) the Department's functions were to be regrouped to place more emphasis on meeting modern urban needs; (2) the Department's regional structure was to be strengthened so that more decisions could be made in the field; (3) strong leadership was to be achieved at the national level by assignment of groups of related programs and functions to each assistant secretary; (4) emphasis was to be given to meshing Department efforts on improving both the physical and social aspects of urban living; and (5) the plan was to permit the Secretary to work effectively with other departments and agencies to deal with urban problems and to improve urban living.

## The Secretary's Total View

The overriding purpose of the Department, the Secretary noted, was to assist in the orderly growth and development of the nation's urban areas. Especially notable, according to Weaver, were the diverse urban problems. The HUD programs, he said, would reflect this diversity.

But a total view of urban development, in the Secretary's opinion, dictated that this complex of programs be directed under a single set of policies and through maximum staff coordination to enable the Office of the Secretary to oversee the broad directions of Department activities. Accordingly, a major feature of the organization plan was the emphasis given the program-planning-budgeting system, which was to be used to measure the effectiveness, in relation to costs, of all programs.

In Washington, each of the assistant secretaries of HUD administers a set of programs and functions. But the assistant secretary's chief role is to represent the Department rather than special groups of programs. His is a staff as well as a line administrative responsibility, and he participates in the activities of the entire Department.

In terms of line authority, which derives from his appointment by the President with the approval of the Senate, the HUD Secretary, backed by his under secretary, exercises three

## Chart 1
## DEPARTMENT OF HOUSING AND URBAN DEVELOPMENT, OVER-ALL ORGANIZATION

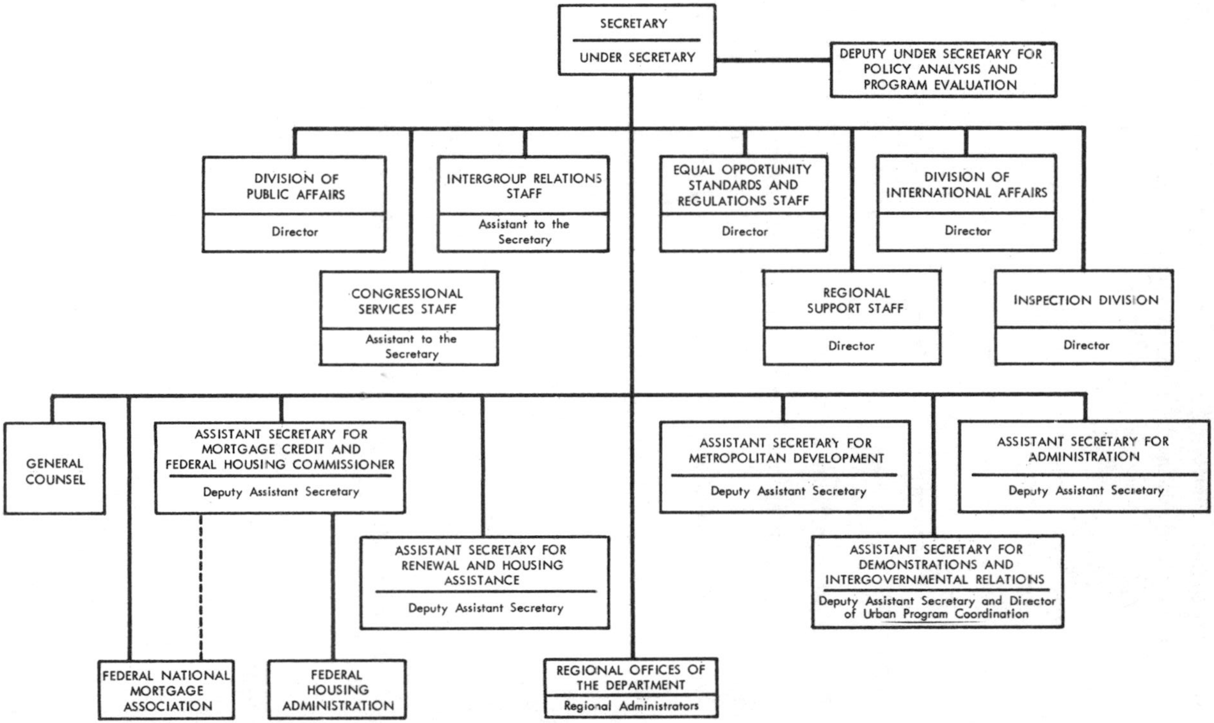

SECRETARY
UNDER SECRETARY

DEPUTY UNDER SECRETARY FOR POLICY ANALYSIS AND PROGRAM EVALUATION

DIVISION OF PUBLIC AFFAIRS
Director

INTERGROUP RELATIONS STAFF
Assistant to the Secretary

CONGRESSIONAL SERVICES STAFF
Assistant to the Secretary

EQUAL OPPORTUNITY STANDARDS AND REGULATIONS STAFF
Director

DIVISION OF INTERNATIONAL AFFAIRS
Director

INSPECTION DIVISION
Director

REGIONAL SUPPORT STAFF
Director

ASSISTANT SECRETARY FOR ADMINISTRATION
Deputy Assistant Secretary

ASSISTANT SECRETARY FOR METROPOLITAN DEVELOPMENT
Deputy Assistant Secretary

ASSISTANT SECRETARY FOR DEMONSTRATIONS AND INTERGOVERNMENTAL RELATIONS
Deputy Assistant Secretary and Director of Urban Program Coordination

ASSISTANT SECRETARY FOR MORTGAGE CREDIT AND FEDERAL HOUSING COMMISSIONER
Deputy Assistant Secretary

ASSISTANT SECRETARY FOR RENEWAL AND HOUSING ASSISTANCE
Deputy Assistant Secretary

REGIONAL OFFICES OF THE DEPARTMENT
Regional Administrators

FEDERAL HOUSING ADMINISTRATION

FEDERAL NATIONAL MORTGAGE ASSOCIATION

GENERAL COUNSEL

levels of supervision and direction. His own operation includes officers in charge of public affairs, Congressional services, intergroup relations, equal opportunity standards and regulations, regional support, international affairs, and inspection. Also reporting directly to the Secretary and his under secretary, is a deputy under secretary for Policy Analysis and Program Evaluation.

The HUD Secretary's most potent level of control is in the highly important program teams, which include Mortgage Credit (FHA and FNMA), Renewal and Housing Assistance, Metropolitan Development, and Demonstrations and Intergovernmental Relations, all headed by assistant secretaries appointed by the Secretary. (See chapters IV, V, VI, and VII for details of programs.) In addition, there is an assistant secretary for Administration and a general counsel. The former handles major management, organization, and staffing matters for the Secretary, and the counsel's office is concerned with the legalities involving the Department and all of its programs.

The HUD Secretary has a direct line of authority to the regional offices, where the structure is something of a miniature of the Secretary's office. A regional administrator and his deputy have assistants for the major programs handled by assistant secretaries at the national level and, also, staff for special functions.

While he was awaiting word from President Johnson in late 1965 and early 1966 on whether he would be the man to take over as Secretary of the Department of Housing and Development—the job that he had been filling on an interim basis as the former HHFA chief—Robert Clifton Weaver once confided: "I feel like a woman who waited nine months—and nothing happened." During the long, pregnant months that finally resulted in his official appointment and confirmation, Weaver started to build the team that is now leading the HUD effort.

The first HUD Secretary was born in Washington, D.C., on

December 29, 1907. He graduated from the District's then segregated Dunbar High School and, subsequently, from Harvard, where he later earned his M.A. and Ph.D. in economics. The author of four books on city problems and widely experienced in local, state, and national government, he is an effective public speaker, who can avoid stepping on too many toes. Erudite without being pedantic and warm without being effusive, both as HHFA chief and as HUD Secretary, he has shuffled personnel without being regarded as an uprooter—even while making major changes and taking some prestige away from FHA and FNMA.

Weaver has, of course, been criticized—as "a dreamer and theoretician who fails to appreciate the numbers significance (money involved) in vast programs," and as a dedicated but overcautious career man who has "learned the government ropes and how not to burn his hands while climbing them." Certainly, he made history on the day that he was appointed to the Cabinet, becoming the first Negro in the United States to sit at the President's executive table. One of his friends, who worked with him during the HHFA period, has insisted that it is realistic to appraise the appointment itself as the major achievement in Weaver's life and not unkind to think of him as "playing his HUD role academically and as safely as possible to preserve, rather than enhance, his role in history."

With such interest groups as the National Association of Real Estate Boards and the National Association of Home Builders, Weaver's low-key approach has served well, in that he has raised no personal hackles. (However, many realtors roundly criticized the Department, and Weaver as the head of it, for what the NAHB considered too little, too late concern for the depressed state of the home-building industry and its mortgage money problems in 1966.)

As his number two man, Weaver chose Robert C. Wood, who was chairman of the political science department at Massachusetts Institute of Technology before joining the HUD team in January, 1966. Like Weaver, a scholar, an author, and a man of extensive experience in government service, Wood had played a large role in the White House task force that shaped the new Department in which he was named under secretary.

Some of Wood's outlook can be understood from what he said in a speech he made shortly after his appointment:

> As contemporary problems such as poverty, social disorganization, civil rights and rampant urbanization become identified, creative federalism responds with solutions. This development, still in evolution, parallels what is happening in the defense and space industries. These are today vast complexes of private and public enterprise, contiguous in their operation at many different points but ordered systematically within the context of specific problems to be solved.

## Reorganization of Forces

In order to unify and control the direction of the new Department's field activities in mid-1966, Secretary Weaver signed orders to provide what he called an administrative framework for directing the interrelated programs of the Department toward the same major purposes. His orders:

Transferred, to the Department's regional offices, the housing assistance regional offices and changed delegations and reporting lines to reflect the regional administrators' responsibility for supervision of the housing assistance programs, with the housing assistance offices to be headed by assistant regional administrators reporting to the Department's regional administrators;

Established, in the Department's regional offices, assistant regional administrators for FHA, reporting to the Department regional administrators, with responsibility for reviewing FHA project proposals having a relationship to other programs of the Department;

Established, in the Department's regional offices, a new

program coordination and services division, headed by an assistant regional administrator reporting to the regional administrator. This division was to perform functions relating to comprehensive planning, workable programs, economic and market analysis, and relocation, and provide the regional administrator and his deputy with the strong capability needed to assure program coordination.

Central to the challenges facing HUD at all levels was—and is—its federal mandate to assist in the solution of urban problems by improving existing programs and developing new ones so that all federal activities in housing and urban development operate as levers that multiply the benefits of private, state, and municipal actions in the field. The primary mission of the new Department was—and is—to carry out major functions relating to the improvement of the physical environment of the urban community and to provide a focus for the coordination of related executive branch efforts.

A HUD report, in late 1966, to the Subcommittee on Executive Reorganization of the Senate Committee on Government Operations summed up some organizational temptations to be avoided:

> The prior history of the housing agencies had fully illustrated the danger of assigning governmental functions, except as a temporary expedient, primarily on the basis of technical skills. Such an assignment may make it possible for a new program to be started more quickly and to be operated more economically in its earlier years. However, the long-range disadvantages are overwhelming, as your subcommittee has pointed out. Technicians who are more familiar with the *how* than the *why* of a program tend, out of concern with narrowly defined efficiency, to resist desirable changes of direction. Sometimes, like the fanatic of the epigram, they redouble their efforts when they have forgotten their aims.

The same report noted that a "quiet organizational revolution" in the field of urban affairs had started some years ago and has been proceeding at an accelerating rate.

*Special Status of FHA*

In looking at the HUD structure, it is essential to recall that Congress—at the behest of private housing groups—had been adamant about assigning special status to the Federal Housing Administration. It was written into the law establishing the Department that the FHA would retain its separate identity under a commissioner who would be an assistant secretary and who would also handle, under the direction of the HUD Secretary, all other Department programs relating to the private mortgage money market. This action might be seen as having prevented any possibility of FHA having its name, programs, and functions changed or assimilated (as happened with the Public Housing and Urban Renewal administrations).

Thus, today, the assistant secretary for Mortgage Credit is also the Federal Housing commissioner, bearing the Department's mortgage credit responsibilities in the private housing field and the principal functions involved in the programs of FHA and the still somewhat independent FNMA. This assistant secretary is charged with bringing together and strengthening all the tools of the Department that serve the private housing market and with making them more effective in line with the over-all federal objectives in urban development.

Not only was FHA status preserved by the HUD law itself. It is also important to note that Philip N. Brownstein was the only member of the top HHFA, pre-HUD power structure, other than Secretary Weaver himself, to be assigned a major role in the new Department. After serving several years as FHA commissioner, Brownstein was named assistant secretary for Mortgage Credit, still is the FHA boss, and now bears some administrative responsibility for FNMA. (See Chapter IV, and Charts 3 and 4.) During his tenure in FHA before it became part of HUD, as since then, Brownstein's reputation as a solid administrator, able to listen to outside business interests—in his case, the home-building and mortgage industries—without losing perspective or endangering federal solidarity, has been useful. During the mortgage interest escalation of 1966, Brownstein early recognized the desirability of increasing FHA loan rates to keep them competitive. However, he maintained a façade of silence while awaiting approval of HUD and the White House before exercising his authority to increase the FHA rate on mortgage loans. The man who took over FNMA along with FHA, Assistant Secretary Brownstein, in 1967 won a Civil Service League award as one of the ten top careerists in the U.S. Government.

J. Stanley Baughman served as president of FNMA from 1950 until his resignation at age 69, at the end of 1966, and saw the agency become the world's largest mortgage banking facility. He was given the President's Award for Distinguished Federal Civilian Service in 1962.

Raymond H. Lapin of San Francisco was named president of FNMA in June, 1967. A former mortgage banker, Lapin had been commissioner of the California State Economic Development Agency.

## Renewal and Housing Assistance: Two Into One

The two long-standing federal programs in Urban Renewal and Public Housing were combined in the new Department into the Office of the Assistant Secretary for Renewal and Housing Assistance, which administers central-city-oriented programs, notably urban renewal, low-rent public housing, neighborhood and park facilities and beautification, and special types of housing assistance, including loans for rehabilitation and for housing of the elderly.

In choosing a man to replace former Urban Renewal Commissioner William Slayton and Public Housing Administrator Marie McGuire (now in housing for aged under the new assistant secretary), Secretary Weaver selected Don Hummel, former mayor of Tucson, Arizona, who had been in the Office of Price Administration during the early years of World War II, and been assistant U.S. attorney for the Arizona District from 1947 to 1951, and, germane to his urban renewal responsibility, also had served as president of the National League of Cities and of the League of Arizona Cities and Towns.

Marie C. McGuire, who had been named Public Housing administrator by President Kennedy in 1961, found her position downgraded in the HUD reorganization. Mrs. McGuire had been the first woman to occupy the top Public Housing post, created when the low-rent program was established in 1937. She had specialized in public housing for 23 years, serving as executive director of the San Antonio (Texas) Housing Authority for 12 years before taking the top federal post. However, her influence had waned, and, in the new set-up, she was named acting Housing Assistance administrator under the assistant secretary for Renewal and Housing Assistance, before being shifted again. (See Chapter V and Chart 5.)

*New Metropolitan Portfolio*

The assistant secretary for Metropolitan Development holds a totally new housing portfolio within HUD. He is responsible for present and proposed programs affecting urban areas and their expanding, adjacent populated regions. Included in this jurisdiction are many important programs dealing with basic urban planning, water and sewer facilities, outlying open space, urban mass transportation demonstration and research, support of planned community development, and the execution of sound metropolitan planning at the local level. (See Chapter VI, and Chart 6.)

Charles M. Haar joined HUD early in 1966 as assistant secretary for Metropolitan Development. At the time of his appointment, he was a member of the faculty of Harvard Law School, the Littauer School of Public Administration at Harvard, and also a member of the faculty committee of the Joint Center for Urban Studies of Harvard and MIT. Haar practiced real estate, tax, and corporate law in New York and Boston before joining the Harvard faculty, and he has taught courses in land reform for underdeveloped countries, land use planning, real estate transactions, trusts, and realty taxation.

In 1964, Haar was chairman of President Johnson's Task Force on the Preservation of Natural Beauty and, prior to his HUD appointment, had been serving on the President's Task Force on Urban Affairs and Housing. Earlier he had advised President Kennedy on urban problems.

### "Model Cities" Assistant Secretary

Before being called to serve HUD as assistant secretary for Demonstrations and Intergovernmental Relations, H. Ralph Taylor was president of Taylor-Hurley Associates and H. R. Taylor Management Corporation in New York City. Specializing in urban renewal and development, he had been responsible for the programing and development of nearly $100 million of new housing in urban renewal areas since 1959.

Taylor's career had also included a stint with the Agency for International Development, on urban renewal for the government of Chile, and service as vice-chairman of the executive committee of the National Association of Redevelopment Officials. He directed the Redevelopment Agency in New Haven, Connecticut, from 1955 to 1959, and earlier, held a housing authority post in Somerville, Massachusetts, where he supervised the first urban renewal project in that state.

As the assistant secretary for Demonstrations (Model Cities) and Intergovernmental Relations, he now provides the generating force for innovation and experimental development. That role also means working with urban areas in developing and implementing plans to rebuild blighted areas. His intergovernmental role is both broad and highly relevant to the new federalism. (See Chapter VII, and Chart 7.)

### Assistant Secretary for Administration

Although his office bears no program responsibility, the assistant secretary for Administration is regarded as of key importance in the new Department, affecting the operating efficiency of all programs and offices. The assistant secretary directs the management function of the Department, including budget, personnel, accounting, general services, and audits. For this job, Secretary Weaver chose Dwight A. Ink, on the basis of his record of attainment and broad experience in government as assistant general manager of the Atomic Energy Commission and economist with the Bureau of Reclamation.

The choice for the post in Administration reflects a tendency to depend on career men from predecessor or related agencies to fill the high-level positions in the new Department, although talented architects and sociologists from outside government have also been called in. And it is interesting to note that five

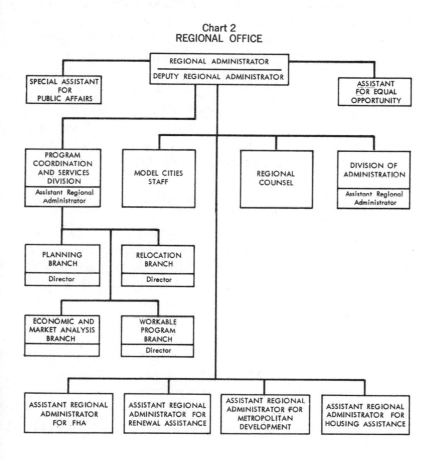

Chart 2
REGIONAL OFFICE

of the men given important assignments in the new HUD had had careers in home building, allied associations, or mortgage banking as background for entry into federal housing jobs. Occasionally, there is some shuffling in medium-level posts between federal housing agencies and the National Association of Home Builders.

One of the responsibilities of the assistant secretary for Administration that is most meaningful, is staffing. Announced projections for increasing the HUD staff above its present 14,000 level indicated that 1,800 to 2,000 new personnel are anticipated in the year ending June 30, 1968. Some of those will be appointed to top positions. HUD hopes to benefit from the new emphasis colleges and universities are giving to urban-oriented programs of studies designed to meet the shortages of trained urban planners and other professionals needed at local, state, and national government levels.

## IN THE FIELD

In the field, Weaver has placed what he called "clear and unambiguous authority" in each new regional administrator— the spokesman for the Department in the field and the coordinator of all of the Department's established programs in the region. All persons responsible for program operations in the region are responsible to him.

The Secretary also has made the regional administrator the channel through which contacts are transmitted between central office and the field. More important, the regional official has the authority to make decisions in most of the HUD programs on the basis of his stature at the high-level Civil Service rating appropriate for an official of his responsibility. As part of HUD's consolidation program for regional offices, heretofore separate regional operations were merged into a single HUD Regional Office for common policy and direction of major programs in relation to communities and states.

For instance, formerly separate Public Housing regional offices were absorbed into the newly reorganized HUD Regional offices, as were the major multifamily responsibilities of FHA, Urban Renewal, and Public Facilities. This significant and basic change now puts these responsibilities in HUD regional offices in New York City, Philadelphia, Atlanta, Chicago, Fort Worth, San Francisco, and Puerto Rico. (See Appendix I for local addresses.)

The regional plan provides greater opportunity to use the varied demonstration programs of HUD, with a minimum of field manuals and instructions and a maximum of flexibility in administering the demonstration programs. A small but mobile Washington staff coordinates the programs, with the regional administrator having a key role.

## GENERAL PRINCIPLES OF HUD ORGANIZATIONAL RELATIONSHIPS

The Secretary's Organization Order No. 2 delineated the "general principles governing organizational relationships within the Department" as follows:

> Organizational relationships in a multiprogram department such as HUD are necessarily complex. Charts and orders establish the basis for such relationships; but charts and orders cannot be expected to provide, in themselves, the understanding and discipline needed to make these relationships effective. The organization of the Department contemplates:
>
> Strong national-level program leadership and coordination through the assignment of Assistant Secretaries to head groupings of related functions;
>
> Strong local-level program leadership and coordination through decentralization of operations to Regional Administrators who are fully responsible for such operations within their regions.

Program authority, the order stated, is to be delegated by the Secretary to the assistant secretaries, and by them to the heads of administrations and offices and to regional administrators for such further delegation within their respective units as may be appropriate.

Each official in the chain of delegations holds all of the powers of each of his subordinates. However, Weaver noted that this delegation does not mean that each official should personally exercise all of these powers. The order adds:

> An essential element in organizational discipline is that each official work at his own level—most specifically, that he forego the temptation to make decisions and take actions that are properly the function of a subordinate official.

## Delineation of Responsibilities

The order also delineated the responsibilities of each assistant secretary as (a) the principal adviser to the Secretary and under secretary with respect to a specified group of functions, and as responsible to the Secretary for their administration; and (b) the one who directs and coordinates, on behalf of the Secretary, the Department's activities with respect to these functions.

Without divesting himself of responsibility, the assistant secretary may delegate to the heads of offices and administrations responsible to him. Generally, he will retain in his own immediate office such functions as:

Development and modification of programs to achieve national purposes;

Development and modification of program goals;

Review of program accomplishment in terms of national purposes and program goals;

Program policy guidance to the heads of administrations and offices and the regional administrators;

Program direction and coordination at the Departmental and field levels;

Decisions on specific actions which, because of their national or departmental significance, have not been delegated by him.

Resolution, in collaboration with other assistant secretaries, of program matters involving their responsibilities.

In defining relationships and detailing responsibilities, the HUD Secretary was facing up to the task of coordinating diffuse and disorganized federal programs ranging from sewage disposal research, and the location of new inner city schools, to the design and route of metropolitan freeways. He had no charter to annex established territories; rather, he must find a way to manipulate programs and people to achieve a workable unity. In terms of organizational necessity, he clearly knew what he was about.

In March, 1966, he said:

There are certain functions which in time must be placed in the Department. The problem is now to identify these and encourage the Administration to sponsor reorganization plans to bring them about.

# IV

# Mortgage Credit: FHA and FNMA

In Washington, where federal alphabet agencies are almost as numerous as the pigeons on the limestone-fronted government buildings, both FHA and FNMA are well known. Nationwide, FHA has reached into even the smallest of communities by virtue of its home loan insurance program to become, in more than one sense, a household name to home owners. FNMA is less known outside housing and financial circles because it does not do business with the general public, but where it is known, it has something that few government agencies can boast—a genuine, widely accepted nickname. The initials FNMA, spelled out vocally, sound like "Fannie Mae"—and that is the unofficial trademark name often seen in financial headlines. (A spokesman for FNMA pointed out that nobody seems to know who coined the nickname, "but everybody uses it." It has been spelled "Fanny May" and, among those who knew FNMA's veteran public affairs officer Francis J. Nowak, "Franny Mae." Nowak's informal poll on the choice of a preferred spelling favored Fannie Mae.)

Over the years, both FHA (established in 1934) and FNMA (established in 1938) have worked together closely, although as separate and independent entities. But it is FHA that has been, and still is, synonymous with housing and government. Today, both alphabet agencies are guided from the same office within HUD, that of the assistant secretary for Mortgage Credit, who, as already noted, is also FHA commissioner. Each agency has its own organization (see Charts 3 and 4), but they overlap, support, affect, and, in truth, could scarcely exist without each other. On this point, it is important to recognize that, in terms of long-range effect, the mortgage financing aspect of HUD equally involves the roles of both FHA and FNMA. FHA, working through the suppliers of mortgage funds and private builders to serve individual families, assures home buyers that regulations concerning construction, site planning, etc., will be met and basic standards enforced. The buyer may be checked, too, by having his application reviewed by an FHA office, although he will have no direct contact here. Fannie Mae works behind the scenes, being involved only in ebbs and floods of the mortgage money tides nationally. But providing a market for FHA-insured loans is basic to the FNMA operation.

## How FHA Works

FHA-insured mortgages can be used to pay for building, buying, or refinancing homes. Essential are the buyer's good credit record, a stipulated down payment and closing costs, as well as the ½ per cent per year for FHA mortgage insurance. The down payment may range from about 3 per cent on a $6,000 home to about 15 per cent on one for $35,000. The FHA maximum loan insurance is for $30,000. Interest rates vary, in response to the general market, with the figure going to 6 per cent in 1966 (a tight money year) from 5.25 per cent in early 1965. The legal maximum is 6 per cent, and the FHA regulations specify only limits—not exact rates. Amortization extends up to a maximum of 30 years.

A new house must meet FHA standards, and an existing house must fulfill basic criteria and objectives of the minimum property standards. During construction, an FHA inspector makes visits to the site—checking sizes of posts and beams, among other structural items, as well as the neighborhood. In recent years, Commissioner Brownstein has instituted paperwork changes that have reduced the long-criticized delays that often occurred from the time applications for FHA-insured loans were made to granting. Processing time, generally, has been trimmed from six weeks to one week.

FHA rules forbid a discount (charge) by an approved lender to a home buyer but cannot prevent the lender from asking a borrower to pay such a charge if he is building houses for sale, or a home to live in, or is refinancing a mortgage.

## Its Record to Date

The reputation of the United States as a nation of home owners reflects both the nature of its people and their general prosperity. To an impressive degree, the extent of home-owning today can be attributed to the mortgage-financing leadership and tools made available by the original FHA, which provided philosophical impact in this changed approach to financing that has brought home ownership within the reach of almost all moderate-income and many relatively low-income families.

During the first thirty-two years of its history, FHA provided mortgage insurance on more than 8 million homes—most of them priced under $20,000 and with relatively low down payments and long terms of amortization, enabling buyers to pay the interest and to pay off the principal on a declining basis in low, regular monthly amounts. FHA insurance has often made it reasonable for lenders to advance credit on terms more liberal than those normally available to families of moderate means. At the end of December, 1966, FHA home mortgages on both new and existing homes totaled more than $81 billion. These loans were made by private lending institutions and processed through FHA's widely placed local insuring offices. FHA mortgage insurance also has covered more than 1 million units in multifamily residential buildings. Altogether, FHA mortgage insurance has been used for more than $112 billion in residential construction affecting more than 38 million families.

In addition, FHA has insured financing for over 28 million property improvement (Title I) loans—usually unsecured—

## Chart 3
## FEDERAL HOUSING ADMINISTRATION

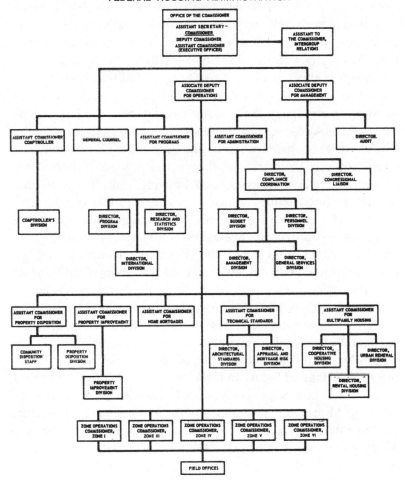

for owners wanting to enlarge, change, maintain, or upgrade their homes.

Over the years, the 9,000-man FHA has been able to boast that it has been self-supporting through income from insurance fees, income, and investments. The insurance reserve fund usually is well in excess of $1 billion. With some pride, too, FHA points out that, of itself, it has built no housing and made no loans. Its principal function has been to issue insurance on mortgage loans made by approved lenders on the basis of FHA's generally pervasive regulations. Recently, the FHA mortgage insurance role has been enlarged, by national legislation, to include land development loans for builder-developers, urban renewal, and housing built for low- and middle-income families at below-market interest rates.

The FHA is credited with revolutionizing home ownership by providing safeguards against the foreclosures on mortgages that were common in the 1930's. FHA foreclosures have been fairly minimal, with an inventory of less than 40,000 usual over the nation.

Although FHA was criticized when it insured mortgages on multifamily dwellings that were poorly located or constructed, it generally has had a favorable press since it first helped the nation build and buy its way out of the economically frustrating 1930's. One of Franklin D. Roosevelt's most pressing problems in his first year as President was the field of private housing. Money for new construction was not easily available, and prospective buyers for planned new homes were scarce. Many existing but mortgaged homes were caught in the rash of foreclosures that scarred many families.

Before the Depression, home owners with bank mortgages, with terms usually up to five years, had been permitted to pay only interest until the term expired. Then, of course, they could be dunned for the full amount. In a period when the banks did not need the money, these home mortgages were usually extended, and owners had little incentive to pay off the principal. The interest payments, usually 6 per cent, were payable annually. When the banks were forced to obtain more liquidity, the pinch on the home owner resulted.

The FHA theory of installment home purchasing, as already noted, is based on insured mortgages with long terms and regular monthly payments of principal and interest. The FHA buyer must meet regulations on credit and income to get a home loan at an interest rate limited by FHA, and he also pays ½ of 1 per cent for the privilege of having the loan insured—an advantage that motivates the lending institutions to make funds available. (Despite precautions, there have been a few flurries of FHA foreclosures—many in Florida where overbuilding in certain areas became a problem, and some new owners walked away from their homes because they had little equity in them.)

Although the FHA rate has fluctuated over the years, usually following the prime rate for money lending, the funds have been made available because FHA takes the risk out of the loan for the lender. Today, FHA-insured buyers can get into a house with a minimum down payment of $200 on a house valued as low as $6,000, or $2,800 on a house with an FHA appraisal of $29,000. The terms can be from ten to thirty years, and these long terms have been a major incentive to buyers. Similar long "payouts" have been adopted by the conventional lenders.

FHA functions have made substantial contributions to the American business community. Among these contributions, many in private industry consider the stabilization factor most important. Because of it, the builder—be he a William J. Levitt or a carpenter who wants to build a single speculative sale house on his own for the first time—can obtain commitments of both construction and mortgage money that mean the house can be built and be sold.

With prospective home buyers, the advantages of FHA-insured financing are so well established that builders of new houses, and sellers of "used" or existing houses, usually signify the FHA possibility in any advertising that may be done. Let there be no misunderstanding. House financing is sold as much as the house. The $25,000 house with an attractive "financing package" sells much faster than an equivalent house for which the buyer has to obtain his own financing. And the word attractive, to a home purchaser, usually means a small down payment and low interest rates over a long amortization. There is no doubt that the FHA has been responsible for the increased number of home buyers in the United States, by fostering a method of financing that makes home purchase almost as easy as paying rent.

FHA financing, or the private long-term credit plan of home buying it has engendered, can be criticized on the basis that the owner of record is little more than a title holder. After making his small down payment with interest, taxes, and insurance premium prepaid, the new owner of record may not even hold his deed. The mortgage holder, or his agent, has a far greater stake in the house. It is usual for the mortgage banker, representing the mortgage holder, to collect a monthly payment from the buyer and then dole out the insurance, interest payments, and reduction of principal and taxes. Thus, the buyer often thinks of himself as something less than an owner.

But if the FHA plan has warranted criticism for breeding home owners who are not really owners at all, it also has been praised for enabling many low- and moderate-income families to budget and save for a small down payment and, having purchased a home, to live frugally while making payments and building up an equity—slow as that may be in the early years of a long-term mortgage.

As a means of enforced saving, the installment purchase of a home has enabled many owners to build up an equity that, even within five to ten years, strengthens their personal financial position to the extent that the home purchased when children are small can often be sold for a profit and the money realized can be used as a down payment for a larger, newer model more suited to the needs of a larger or more mature family.

FHA-style, pay-as-you-live-in-it home financing also enables ownership changes to be made readily. Although not many homes are on wheels (and even the so-called mobile homes are seldom moved these days), the U.S. dwelling has become part of a highly mobile society, in which one of every five families moves every year.

Over the last thirty years, FHA has enabled many millions of Americans to become home owners. And the agency has also been enlarged to do many more things. Title I loans for property improvements have enabled owners of deteriorating or outdated homes to borrow up to $3,500 for five years on the basis of personal, unsecured loans with FHA insurance. Responsibility for credit approval or disapproval is delegated by the FHA commissioner to insured lenders. Other Title I loans up to $3,500 can be used to finance the building of non-residential structures. Mortgage insurance for dwellings that house more than one family has been made available. Other provisions aid home owners who have suffered property losses in natural disasters and renovators of one-to-four family dwellings for the displaced.

## Broadened Programs

In 1965, the broadened scope of FHA was recognized by the Congress, which provided the controversial rent supplement program and also new insurance for land development mortgages.

Rent supplements were designed to "lift the curtain of poverty," according to FHA Commissioner Brownstein, who noted that poor families in need of adequate housing had been barred financially from private housing developments. Under the rent supplement program, FHA insures mortgages at a market rate of interest for sponsors that can be nonprofit organizations, cooperatives, or limited dividend groups. Projects are constructed by private builders and normal tenant-landlord relationships prevail after construction. However, occupancy is limited to those individuals whose incomes are at or below public housing admission levels. The rent supplement program requires the tenant to pay only 25 per cent of his family income as rent, and the difference between that amount and the actual rent set by the landlord, with FHA approval, is paid by the federal government to the landlord. Funded in 1966, the program attracted sufficient interest to submit a budgetary request for an additional $40 million to contract for approximately 44,500 rent supplement housing units early in 1967. The House turned down this request. However, although there may be no new funds for some time, the program will continue. About 1,500 units (or families) are already getting aid, and HUD has $30 million to get the program moving. Much of that sum is authorized for new and rehabilitated projects coming into the market in 1967; by 1968, it is likely that there will be about 5,000 units in operation with present funds. (See Chapter IX for other comment on the rent supplement issue.)

Basic to the FHA program for mortgage insurance on land development was recognition of the statistical impact from an estimated 2 million housing "starts" (beginning of construction) each year through 1975 to provide additional housing for an exploding American population and to keep pace with the replacement housing needs generated by annual losses of existing shelter through razing done on the basis of urban redevelopment and obsolescence. Most of this projected housing expansion is expected to be located within the sphere of metropolitan influence of the nation's largest cities. In order to encourage developers to plan in larger terms on long-range projects, the land development loan insurance provides assistance for land acquisition and holding, on which financing charges can become disastrous to the economic position of builders operating on a tight cash margin.

Another new move came with the agency's decision to consider the income of working wives when qualifying families for FHA home loan insurance. This action recognized the trend for working wives to return to the labor force soon after the birth of a child in order to help maintain the family's standard of living and accepted the wife's income as part of a family's long-range budgeted income.

HUD has noted that new tools are available to overcome financing problems involved in the rehabilitation of slum properties, but they are administered by the Renewal Projects Administration. However, FHA has its own Section 220 insured loans, available for several years, on the basis of prevailing interest, long-term and high-loan ratio found in the home loans. Mortgages on new and existing construction are insured. On new buildings, the maximum loan insurance is for 97 per cent of estimated replacement cost. Interest in the 220 insurance program has been only moderate, with 3,866 mortgages being insured on new houses involving 4,040 living units and 646 mortgages on existing home properties with 1,365 living units —as of the end of 1966. On multifamily housing structures, involving 69,778 units, there were 212 mortgages insured on new projects and 47 on existing projects with 1,575 living units. This 220 section has been in effect since 1954.

A lack of interest in those FHA-insured loans for new construction and rehabilitation influenced the Congress to augment rehabilitation financing plans in the Housing Act of 1964. Under its Section 312, administered by the Urban Projects Administration, a low-interest, long-term direct loan was set up to be administered by the Local Planning Authority, in conjunction with the Urban Renewal Administration (then a separate HHFA entity but now part of the HUD complex of Renewal and Housing Assistance programs discussed in Chapter V). These direct loans are made to individual owners and sometimes to tenants on the basis of 3 per cent interest with terms up to 20 years for a maximum of $10,000 per living unit or $50,000 per property.

Usable on residential or commercial properties, Section 312 loans may be first or second mortgages. Loans under $3,500 may not require a mortgage. FHA processes those for amounts over $3,500 for the local public agency on a reimbursement basis. Also, an owner-occupant of an existing building with four or fewer units may refinance existing loans to keep housing expenses in a reasonable ratio to income.

These loans are available on property in approved urban renewal areas or in approved Section 117 code enforcement areas. The loans are made in clearance areas, for instance, on properties that are labeled "spot rehabilitation" or "not to be acquired."

The main purpose of Section 312 loans is to bring the property up to the applicable minimum code or property rehabilitation standard. However, loans also may be used for nonluxury items that contribute to the livability—if considered to be typical for the neighborhood. The only restriction is that the items do not constitute overimprovement of the general neighborhood pattern.

The processing of an individual loan application is not subject to origination processing by an outside party. Rather, origination is the function of the local planning authority or city agency designated to perform those details.

Some of the functions concerned with the applications include interviewing and counseling property owners, preparing the report of work required, obtaining credit reports and exhibits, getting bids from contractors, providing prior appraisals of the property, verification of ownership, and preparation of the loan application.

The total loan application information is forwarded to the new rehabilitation loan section of the regional HUD office where a rehabilitation loan officer is assigned. If approved, the project gets a commitment to proceed. Then the local planning authority helps the property owner to let a contract, conducts inspections during construction, orders the loan check from HUD, sets up the terms of loans and fund disbursement, and finally returns the papers to HUD.

Monthly payment collections are handled by a local lending institution that enables the property owner to make his payments on a regular schedule. All through the many procedures, the owner and the local authorities have the assistance and advice of HUD officials.

The Section 312 loan standards are not as rigid, but nonetheless are generally similar, to those for FHA Section 220 loans. However, there are buildings that are physically unfeasible for rehabilitation. A structure, for instance, could be substandard and remain so even after being rehabilitated. The main target in the 312 program is toward originally sound buildings that have grown old or rundown but have a potential for rehabilitation that would be less expensive than razing and rebuilding.

If a project has fifty or more properties to be rehabilitated, it is often placed with a full-time financial adviser, who can be added to the local planning agency staff. He may be an important member of the staff, performing a variety of roles—including public relations and technical assistance on obtaining mortgages and loans.

Of an entirely different nature, but particularly interesting, is the authorization of a direct grant to an owner-occupant of a small property within an approved urban renewal area or code enforcement boundary. The grant may cover the cost of repairs needed to bring the property up to standard, with the maximum government gift being $1,500.

To be eligible for such a grant, the applicant must own and occupy the premises and the local authority must determine that he qualifies under the hardship factor to avoid displacement. Certain income levels are specified for eligibility. For instance, $3,000 is the maximum for a husband and wife. Where income exceeds $3,000, a partial grant may be possible if the ratio of housing expense to total income is favorable. If the cost of the work exceeds $1,500, a Section 312 loan may be obtained. But the grant is not distributed until the loan for the amount over the $1,500 is obtained.

Sometimes, when the additional money is not obtainable from a loan, the local authority is able to get labor donated by a church group or trade school—using the grant itself to cover building materials.

The FHA extension of mortgage insurance to older neighborhoods is a logical extension of previous efforts. The program was begun by insuring mortgages on residential redevelopment within an urban renewal area. More recently, insurance has been made available on experiments in rehabilitation in blighted areas.

In New York City, a widely publicized FHA "instant rehabilitation" project on East 5th Street has served as a showcase of the adaptation of American construction know-how in engineering and prefabrication techniques. Usually applied in the rebuilding of old tenement buildings, the procedure of instant rehabilitation starts with opening a center hole in the old structure and ripping out everything except the load-bearing walls. The next step is to get rid of the trash and then insert prefabricated kitchen-bathroom-heating cores, complete in every detail, and stacked one on top of another, for quick connection. These cores represent the heart of the rehabilitated building.

Rehabilitation projects in New York using similar techniques, and being financed or already completed, under the FHA experimental-housing program include U.S. Gypsum's project on 102d Street, and others on 114th, 100th, and 15th streets. And there are, of course, many more in cities across the country. (See also Chapter X.)

## How Fannie Mae Works

The Federal National Mortgage Association is the mortgage banker for the private mortgage bankers—buying their mortgages when they need new money and selling mortgages to them when they have surplus funds to invest.

Working separately from FHA, but as a complementing facility, FNMA channels borrowed private funds from areas with ample credit to those needing such investment money for the making of FHA and VA loans. FHA is responsible for having supplied the insurance and mortgage provisions that attach national trading value to its mortgage instruments.

Since HUD's creation, the assistant secretary for Mortgage Credit has served also as FHA commissioner, directing all

Chart 4
FEDERAL NATIONAL MORTGAGE ASSOCIATION

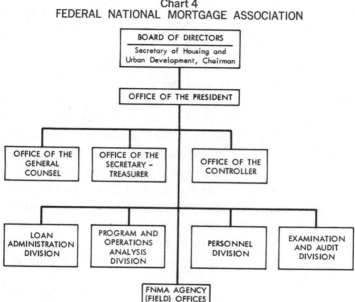

HUD programs involving the private mortgage market and holding responsibility for coordinating the separate activities of FHA and FNMA. Billions of dollars in mortgages are involved annually in the roles of FHA and FNMA, and the United States has developed a vital, powerful mortgage banking industry, which buys and sells and even places loans made by large banks, insurance companies, and other sources of investment funds for both FHA and VA mortgages.

HUD Secretary Weaver serves as chairman of the FNMA Board, and Assistant Secretary Brownstein is a Board member. Regional FNMA offices, in addition to headquarters in Washington, are located in Atlanta, Chicago, Dallas, Los Angeles, and Philadelphia. A sales office is located in New York City to serve the financial marts.

In the field of mortgage credit operations, both within and without the federal framework, this federally chartered corporation of mixed government and private ownership is respected. Completely self-sustaining, it has gained its service reputation by encouraging home ownership through making a broad-based market available for the buying and selling of government-backed home mortgages. So important is this role that the National Association of Home Builders, as well as the National Association of Real Estate Boards, have suggested to HUD that a new central mortgage facility be set up by Fannie Mae to handle conventional home mortgages in similar fashion.

The contributions FNMA has made to the nation's economy have been recognized for many years. In 1963, on the occasion of its twenty-fifth anniversary, President John F. Kennedy said: "Its program of purchase and sale of residential mortgages has been a striking example of how government and industry can cooperate to accomplish most worthwhile results in our economy."

That service to the economy began in 1938, when Sam H. Husbands became the first FNMA president. He served until 1946.

The development of Fannie Mae is interwoven in the nation's economic history from the Depression to this morning's headlines about the world of finance. Lessons learned in the experiments of the years 1932–38, before FNMA was set up, provided some of the foundation for the present agency, which is now the foremost stabilizing force in the market for FHA and VA mortgages. Fannie Mae contributed to the early success of the FHA mortgage insurance program and to that of the VA program instituted in the late 1940's, by providing a secondary market for these types of mortgages and thus encouraging lenders to make the loans.

Fannie Mae was incorporated under federal law on February 10, 1938, four years after the creation of the Federal Housing Administration. Initially chartered as a subsidiary of the Reconstruction Finance Corporation, it was transferred to the Housing and Home Finance Agency in 1950, and, as we have seen, to the Department of Housing and Urban Development in 1965.

Fannie Mae works to assist a home financing industry that may be enjoying a feast of abundant funds one day, a famine the next. This industry is subject to an uneven geographical distribution of investment funds and, in "tight money" periods, is a perennial victim of a run-off of funds—ordinarily available for mortgage loans—to other investments having more attractive returns.

For this mercurial industry, Fannie Mae has been described as acting as a backstop, a balancing wheel, a behind-the-scenes assistant. Whatever the term, its operations have a number of direct and indirect benefits to home financing and the public. Here are some of them:

By assuring lending institutions of a measure of future liquidity in the disposal of residential mortgages, Fannie Mae encourages lenders to commit additional funds for housing loans notwithstanding their long terms.

By adding federal funds—and, more importantly, tapping sources of private funds that would not otherwise be available for residential financing, including funds borrowed on the private capital market—Fannie Mae channels substantial additional credit into housing.

In its national operations, Fannie Mae funnels funds borrowed from capital surplus areas into capital shortage areas, and, thus, is an instrument for piping credit into geographical areas where it is needed most.

By purchasing mortgages during credit shortage periods and selling them during credit surplus periods, Fannie Mae reduces the adverse effects on the residential lending and construction industries of alternate periods of credit shortage and surplus.

By pioneering in the purchase of newer classes of mortgages or by providing more favorable purchase terms for special classes of mortgages, Fannie Mae provides housing credit so as to serve important public purposes.

In its early development, Fannie Mae was effective in blazing the trail in new forms of home financing and channeling credit into home lending. Up through mid-1954, for the most part, it used funds borrowed directly or indirectly from the government to purchase mortgages. Despite the success of this technique, housing and home finance groups saw the need for a broader operation, primarily financed with private funds, to provide a secondary market facility for home mortgages. This extended facility, it was proposed, eventually would be privately owned.

In response to recommendations of the trade groups and those of a Presidential advisory committee, Congress, in 1954, rechartered Fannie Mae, reorganizing it into the present corporation with three distinct operations, including the secondary market operations—an entirely new financing concept.

### Secondary Market Operations

The "new" Fannie Mae's secondary market operation is capitalized with preferred stock held by the Secretary of the Treasury and common stock held by the public, and it issues funds to mortgage sellers and those borrowing from the Association on the security of mortgages. Its financing comes principally from borrowings from the public; it has produced steady earnings over the years; it pays the equivalent of federal corporate income taxes; and it is established so that it may eventually be turned over to the common stockholders.

The principal objective of this operation is to help provide liquidity for mortgage investments and improve the distribution of investment capital available for home financing—in the main, through the purchase of FHA and VA mortgages from private lending institutions. It also sells such mortgages to private investors. Generally, its purchases are greatest during periods of credit stringency, and its sales largest in abundant money periods.

From 1954 through the end of 1966, this operation purchased 666,921 mortgages for $8 billion, and sold 199,571 mortgages for $2.3 billion. In the severe tight-money period of 1966, it bought a record-breaking $2 billion worth of FHA and VA mortgages. Its largest sales year was 1963 when $780 million in mortgages were sold. In each of these years, this operation dramatically demonstrated its value to home financing—in 1966, by supplying acutely needed additional mortgage credit, and earlier, in the abundant year of 1963, by providing well-seasoned mortgage investments for private investors with excess investable funds.

## Special Assistance Function

A second Fannie Mae operation is its special assistance function which operates in much the same way as did the "old" Fannie Mae—using funds borrowed from the government to finance selected types of home mortgages that qualify under special government programs. Such special assistance provides more liberal mortgage purchase terms than prevail in the Association's regular secondary market operations. Over the years since 1954, programs receiving such assistance have been disaster housing, defense housing, veterans' housing, experimental housing, housing in urban renewal areas, housing for persons displaced by urban renewal activities, housing for the elderly, and housing for those of low or moderate incomes, including housing assisted by below-market interest rate mortgages and rent supplements.

## Management and Liquidating Function

Fannie Mae's third mortgage operation is its management and liquidating function, under which it liquidates mortgages the Association purchased under the old Fannie Mae prior to November, 1954.

## The Tally

Fannie Mae's indirect aid to home financing over the years has been incalculable, for there is no measure of how many private loans were made as a result of the FNMA's presence in the market as a "backstop." However, its substantial direct benefit to residential financing is measurable by its record of mortgage purchases and sales. These transactions are given below by mortgage operations—Secondary Market Operations (SMO), Special Assistance Functions (SAF), and Management and Liquidating Functions (M&L) from November, 1954, through the end of 1966.

| Operation | Purchases | | Sales | |
|-----------|-----------|-----------|-----------|-----------|
| | Number | Amount(*) | Number | Amount(*) |
| SMO | 666,921 | $8,044 | 199,571 | $2,336 |
| SAF | 140,050 | 2,779 | 31,178 | 666 |
| M&L | 705,751 | 5,714 | 324,260 | 2,114 |
| Total | 1,512,722 | 16,537 | 555,009 | 5,116 |

* Amounts in millions of dollars.

### Additional New Operations

Fannie Mae received a new bonnet in 1964. It was assigned an added function, not related to its traditional mortgage operations. Under a statute of that year, the Association was designated to administer a government participation financing program. The program was designed as a vehicle for substituting private for government financing of certain government-held assets to conserve federal budget resources.

In administering the program, Fannie Mae, as trustee, sells to dealers, for resale to the public, certificates of participation in pools of government assets. Initially, the assets were government-financed mortgages held by Fannie Mae and the Veterans Administration.

Later, in 1966, the program was expanded to allow a total of six governmental departments and agencies to establish pools of their assets for this type of financing. They are: the Farmers Home Administration of the Department of Agriculture; the Office of Education of the Department of Health, Education, and Welfare; the Department of Housing and Urban Development; the Veterans Administration; the Export-Import Bank; and the Small Business Administration.

Since inauguration of the program in 1964, and through early 1967, Fannie Mae has sold a total of $4.1 billion in certificates of participation in trusts established under this program.

Fannie Mae also plays a role in the Demonstration (Model) Cities and Metropolitan Development Act of 1966. Its special assistance powers enable FNMA to provide financing help for new community land development mortgages insured by FHA under Title X; to participate up to 95 per cent in making FHA-insured construction loans on cooperative housing, under Section 213; urban renewal projects, under Section 220; and housing for low- and moderate-income families, under Section 221(d)(3).

Also, FNMA now is empowered to commit to purchase and to purchase below-market interest rate mortgages insured under Section 221(h) to finance the rehabilitation of deteriorating or substandard housing for subsequent resale to low-income purchasers. The mortgage must cover at least five individual dwellings, but they need not be contiguous. FNMA also is authorized to purchase mortgages on rent supplement projects. Those purchases are limited to market interest rate mortgages insured by FHA under Section 221(d)(3).

Both FNMA and FHA retain their pre-HUD importance as their activities expand under the Department. Some of the new directions these cooperating parts of the whole administered by the assistant secretary for Mortgage Credit may be expected to take are discussed in the concluding chapters of this book.

# V

# Renewal and Housing Assistance

Prior to the establishment of HUD, two of the major constituent agencies of HHFA were the Urban Renewal Administration and the Public Housing Administration.

It is considered significant that HUD abolished the Public Housing Administration and the post of Public Housing commissioner along with the Urban Renewal Administration and its commissioner. Now, those functions are handled under the assistant secretary for Renewal and Housing Assistance, who also has responsibility for the community programs and housing for "senior citizens." This change was made in an effort to get more comprehensive treatment of the projects within individual frameworks. Deputy secretaries now handle renewal, and housing assistance. And there are directors, or special assistants, for special housing assistance, urban neighborhood services, housing for the elderly and handicapped, and workable program standards and services.

The assistant secretary's principal concern relates to HUD's over-all effort to make central cities better places to live. Assistant Secretary Hummel, first man named for the combined program, described housing as the primary objective "and renewal as the rejuvenating process."

Almost all of the nation's new population growth has been based on urban centers, which need more streets, bigger water systems, more sewage disposal mains, and other facilities to serve expanding populations. All Americans have become increasingly aware that large cities are overcrowded, and that

Chart 5
ASSISTANT SECRETARY FOR RENEWAL AND HOUSING ASSISTANCE

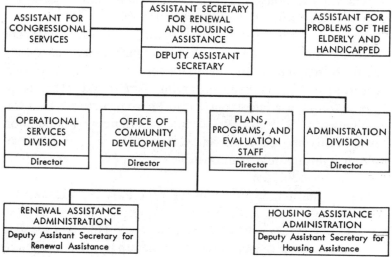

many residential buildings and public facilities grow shoddy and tired in old age.

In addition, greater emphasis is being directed to the need for parks and playgrounds within and around large cities. Both local and national efforts are under way to achieve cleaner air and more adequate and modern public transportation facilities.

Meanwhile, it has been recognized that the elderly, the poor, and the handicapped have had difficulty finding suitable homes that they can afford within the metropolitan areas of their choosing. Thus, HUD's renewal and housing assistance program is being tailored to help solve urban troubles through renewal, low-rent public housing, park and beautification programs, home loan "fix-up" programs, and community building incentives.

Late in 1966, HUD reorganized the urban renewal and public housing operations to include communitywide development services within a new Office of Community Development. This responsibility now includes relocation and social planning and services for all HUD programs, the community design aspects of renewal and housing assistance programs, and, also, workable programs for community improvement.

During a 1966 visit to Wilmington, Delaware, Assistant Secretary Hummel noted that that city typifies many of the urban problems that are the dominant concern of HUD and, particularly, of his combined programs. Not unlike other large cities, Wilmington lost about 15,000 residents from its central area between 1950 and 1960, while experiencing a population boom in surrounding towns and suburban areas. Today, metropolitan Wilmington accounts for more than 80 per cent of little Delaware's population.

One of the new federal housing programs provides aid for concentrated code enforcement. A grant of more than $500,000 was approved for Wilmington's Hilltop East and East Side sections to enable the city to set up housing and building code enforcement programs to bring substandard dwellings up to basic living levels. Work on individual homes is done by private building contractors on the basis of grants or loans made through HUD.

Other new federal programs include the leasing of private housing, acquisition and rehabilitation of private housing, and the construction of public housing by private builders on a contract, or "turnkey" basis to save time and money. In addition, grants are made for neighborhood facilities for health, recreation, education, and related services directed to the needs of low-income families. Direct loans and grants provide for the rehabilitation of properties owned by low-income families, demolition of buildings regarded as hazards to health and safety, rent supplements for privately built housing for lower income families, and grants for urban beautification in the form of parks, playgrounds, and open spaces.

The low-rent public housing program of HUD is now working on a schedule of 60,000 new units a year. About half of

The first home insured by FHA—in Pompton Plains, New Jersey—was purchased in 1934.

This single-family house in Bellevue, Washington, received an FHA honor award for residential design in 1963.

Liberty Square Housing Project, New Haven, Connecticut, which won an FHA design award in 1964. The project houses low- and middle-income families and is financed with a below-market interest rate FHA-insured mortgage.

River Park Townhouses in Washington, D.C., a joint venture of the Reynolds Metals Company and the Redevelopment Land Agency, is the first cooperative community in the Southwest Washington urban renewal area.

Kips Bay Plaza, New York. This 1,120-unit project won an FHA design award in 1964.

FHA-insured student housing at Western Washington State College.

These Baltimore, Maryland, brick row houses were rehabilitated with private financing under FHA's Section 220 program, which is keyed for use in formal urban renewal and code enforcement areas.

These three buildings in New York's Lower East Side were chosen for the 48-hour rehabilitation experiment financed by FHA.

Workmen attach cables to preassembled kitchen-bathroom to be lifted to roof and lowered into position.

Workmen prepare to lower the unit into the building. Instructions are given to the crane operator by radio.

This tenement on Harlem's East 102d Street was one of six blighted buildings selected for U.S. Gypsum's urban rehabilitation program, the first time an American corporation engaged in urban renewal.

Building as it looks now.

Before urban renewal, Philadelphia's historic Independence Hall was hemmed in by decaying buildings.

Today, Independence Hall opens on to a three-block-long mall (here shown under construction) developed with state and federal funds.

Society Hill's Dock Street, along the Delaware River in Philadelphia, was once the City's food-distribution center.

Apartment buildings rise on the site of the old Dock Street market. This entire area, once a commercial section, has become an area of new and restored eighteenth-century homes. A marina will replace the old river docks.

Model of HUD's new home, adjacent to Washington's L'Enfant Plaza redevelopment area.

HUD Secretary Robert C. Weaver discusses "model city" program for Norfolk, Virginia, with Congressman Porter R. Hardy (left) and Norfolk's Redevelopment Director Lawrence M. Cox.

those residential units will be in new garden or high-rise buildings. Approximately 35,000 units may be provided through cooperation of private enterprise in a new program wherein existing dwellings are leased or garden apartment projects are purchased and then rehabilitated by private contractors.

The "turnkey" approach is bringing private builders, restorers, and redevelopers into the public housing program by enabling them to build an apartment project on a particular site. If the local housing authority is interested, the builder is asked for preliminary plans, specifications, and estimated price. Upon approval, the plans are formalized by the local authority signing a letter of intent to purchase the project if the price is satisfactory. If it is, a contract is signed. Otherwise, the builder is paid for preparing final working plans.

Another phase of builder participation in public housing finds private developers and builders buying slum houses and rehabilitating them for sale to the local public housing authority. Under this scheme, profits can be compared favorably with what the builder-developer might obtain by activity in new house construction. It works to everyone's advantage. In Philadelphia, for example, officials have observed that more units have been made available for less money. The Philadelphia Housing Authority reported that it is buying the rehabilitated houses at an average price of $12,300 and spending $1,700 per unit to administer the program, and pointed out that new units with less space cost about $20,000.

Like FHA, public housing got its start in the 1930's when programs were devised to stimulate construction of low-rent homes for families hard hit by the economic dip. The Housing Act of 1937 authorized the start of public housing. The program changed quickly when World War II produced housing shortages for war workers in areas where housing was limited. Over the years, more than 600,000 units of public housing have been provided to families, most of them refugees from unsanitary or decayed dwellings. The Johnson Administration has said that an additional 300,000 living units have been provided in urban renewal areas. Most of the latter, however, have been for medium- and above-average income residents.

## THE NEW HAVEN STORY

Whenever urban renewal is discussed in housing meetings, the New Haven, Connecticut, program and results are mentioned and often emphasized. New Haven's renewal program covers one-third of its urban area and also involves the largest per capita expenditure of any city in the nation. The result is that old neighborhoods no longer show their age. The new, fresh look sparkles from 8,300 housing units, which have been rehabilitated at a cost of $14 million to owners. Nearly 2,000 of those rehabilitated units were completed in one year, 1965.

Another facet of the New Haven renewal is a $37 million new look in the Oak Street industrial area where sixty-nine modern industrial plants now provide clean working locations for thousands who formerly earned their living in obsolete buildings.

Critics who have castigated federal urban renewal for providing posh apartments and townhouses for the well-to-do on sites where blighted housing had been razed, are often asked to take note of the mix of low-income, middle-class, and luxury living on New Haven renewal sites. More than 330 units were designed for elderly residents in six locations. For all residents, both rental and cooperative ownership are offered.

Some of the nation's foremost architects, including Paul Rudolph, Philip Johnson, and the late Eero Saarinen, are represented in New Haven urban renewal areas, which have won awards in a number of national competitions.

The twelve separate New Haven projects involve more than $113 million of federal grants and fund reservations. This vast investment in physical renewal has been accompanied by a "community progress program," originally funded by the Ford Foundation, that is aimed at human renewal and has been used as a laboratory for many of the tests set up by the federal anti-poverty program. Professionals in search of knowledge of practical urban renewal have come from American cities and countries in all parts of the world to see in New Haven what can be accomplished by a full-scale attack on both blight and poverty. HUD Secretary Weaver has referred to New Haven as "coming closest to the dream of a slumless city."

## FOR COLLEGES AND HOSPITALS

Although, basically, the urban renewal and public housing programs are aimed at helping cities and their people, a distinct HHFA-HUD program now administered in this division of the Department assists colleges and hospitals in expanding their facilities to care for increasing numbers of students and personnel. Loans for college housing must be used for construction of residence halls, faculty and married student housing, dining facilities, college union buildings, and housing for student nurses and interns. Loans may be repaid on terms up to fifty years at an interest rate of 3 per cent. Public or private nonprofit colleges and universities may apply, as may hospitals, on the basis of need and accreditation. Before HUD was born, nearly $3 billion had been reserved for loans to college housing programs and approval had been granted for more than 2,440 specific projects on campuses throughout the land. Those residential units for colleges and hospitals total more than 646,000 in all parts of the United States, Puerto Rico, Guam, and the Virgin Islands.

In Kansas City, Missouri, where total urban renewal programs for approved projects passed the $15 million mark and $20 million more is in the planning stage, nine college housing loans were made to six educational institutions and teaching hospitals. (It should be noted, too, that Kansas City razed its worst "Skid Row" and won HUD approval for 2,373 public housing units.) Primary support for the sweeping urban renewal effort in Kansas City came from organized citizens' groups, the City Council, and the public in general.

## For the Elderly and Handicapped

Good housing for the elderly and the handicapped has been the goal of HUD's programs related to moderate-to-low-income "senior citizens." Federal aid can be approved for low-rent public housing under local housing authorities, or 100 per cent loans to nonprofit sponsors or mortgage insurance for housing citizens in wide ranges of income. FHA insures private lenders against losses on loans.

Americans over sixty-two years of age increased to nearly 23 million in 1965, providing the motivation for the HUD stand that housing programs should sustain the dignity and independence of older citizens. HUD officials also believe that strict formulas and single-minded patterns cannot accomplish its aims for a wide range of housing to suit individual tastes and desires.

Some older citizens seek recreation, but others reject such activity. Almost all are interested in convenient transportation, health and medical services, shopping, and certain religious and educational facilities.

In the three HUD programs geared for older Americans, more than 160,000 housing units have been committed for the elderly, and 112,000 of these residential units have been completed or put under construction in 1966. Completion of projects already reviewed would bring that total to housing for nearly a quarter million persons past age sixty-two.

## Community Improvement

Another broad-range HUD program enables the Secretary to authorize what is called a "workable program for community improvement." This official plan of action for using public and private resources to eliminate and prevent slums and blight is tied to a chart for community growth, and a "workable program" is required as a prerequisite for a locality's eligibility for urban renewal, public housing, and certain FHA mortgage insurance aid. Certification lasts one year and can

be continued on the basis of reported p
ning of 1966, there were 1,289 commun
an active basis or in the application stag

A workable program obtains no feder
does make the community eligible for
clearing, redeveloping, and rehabilitatin
areas; grants for concentrated housing c
ects and those for demolition of unsafe b
FHA mortgage insurance for housing cor
ment in urban renewal areas; Section 22
gage insurance for rental housing for
moderate income and those displaced by
and loans and grants to provide housing
afford standard housing in the private m

Requirements of a workable program
codes and ordinances of sound construc
prehensive community planning with tec
examination of neighborhood resources,
administrative organization to establish g
reaching them, planning and budgeting o
housing for displaced families in the u
provement area, and citizen participation
designated advisory committee.

Meanwhile, the continuing trend to urb
has encouraged HUD to enlarge its role to include aspects of
everyday living. For instance, President Johnson told Congress
on March 2, 1965, that "the problem is people and the quality
of the lives they lead. We want to build not just housing units
but neighborhoods; not just to construct schools but to educate
children; not just to raise income but to create beauty and end
the poisoning of our environment."

Federal grants may be authorized by HUD to local public
bodies and agencies to finance neighborhood facilities needed
for programs carrying out health, recreation, social, or similar
necessary programs of community service.

Particular emphasis on neighborhood facility projects is

placed on locations convenient for use of a significant number of low- and moderate-income families. The projects themselves are often worked out to support a community action program under the Economic Opportunity Act.

The projects include neighborhood or community centers, youth centers, health stations, and other facilities for social services. Grants can cover up to two-thirds of the project cost, or up to 75 per cent in redevelopment areas designated by the Economic Development Administration of the Department of Commerce.

## HUD RELOCATION PROGRAM

In urban renewal projects, families, individuals, and businesses may be displaced when old buildings are razed, when mass transportation is expanded, when open space is created, or when community facilities or public housing programs are initiated.

Under the HUD relocation program, families and individuals may receive up to $200 to cover moving expenses, storage costs, and loss of property. Also, families and elderly persons are entitled to relocation adjustment payments for a limited time if they are not able to obtain public housing.

Businesses or nonprofit organizations are entitled to similar expenses up to $3,000, or reimbursement for actual expenses up to $25,000 may be paid if a locality shares the excess with the federal government. The Small Business Administration can make loans up to twenty years to assist in reestablishment. Relocation payments can also include certain settlement costs incurred in conveying property if reimbursements are not otherwise made.

## BEAUTIFICATION OF CITIES

Beauty within the city is another aspect of the far-reaching HUD programs under the assistant secretary for Renewal and Housing Assistance. The Housing Act of 1965 provided 50 per cent grants to assist communities in carrying out programs for the beautification and improvement of public lands.

These grants may cover up to 50 per cent of the amount by which the cost of the activity is carried out, under an approved program above the usual annual expenditure for comparable activity. Beautification projects are conducted on land owned or controlled by the public and for which there is indication of significant benefits for the community. Examples of such beautification are the development of parks, malls, squares, and public waterfront areas with walks, landscaping, and minor recreation or outdoor exhibition facilities. Street improvements, such as lighting, bench placement, new trees, and decorative paving, also are eligible. One of the first projects completed was a tree-lined shopping mall on F Street in the midtown business area of the nation's capital.

Federal aid also is available for the installation of new, well-designed park furniture and landscaping—but not for the cost of keeping a park clean or better lighted. Rain shelters, sanitary facilities, and kiosks are eligible, whereas golf courses, swimming pools, amphitheaters, and museums are not.

Similar 50 per cent grants are available to help public agencies preserve open space land with value for park, recreation, conservation, scenic, or historic purposes. Grants also may be made to help acquire and clear developed land in built-up areas within a city, if open space need cannot be met in other ways. The locality must have a comprehensive planning program and also an adequate specific program for acquiring and developing open space in the particular urban area.

## THE BROAD VIEW

All told, the HUD interest in renewal and housing assistance covers a broad range of programs and extends into areas of social services, coordination of the problems peculiar to the elderly and the handicapped, and programs that embrace parks and neighborhood facilities for the benefit of all citizens.

Observers of the spread of these activities recall that when the federal program of slum clearance and redevelopment was enacted under Title I of the Housing Act of 1948, federal grants were set up to cover two-thirds of the net cost (or deficit) of clearance and urban renewal projects. A few years later, a broadened program was recommended to combat slums and blight. Within the last decade, new programs and expanded old programs have given localities more working tools to arrest and remove blight—and to meet the needs of people living in the blighted areas.

When tallied during HUD's first year of operation, there were 1,994 Title I grant reservations in 842 localities for a total project value exceeding $5.268 billion. Of that number, the urban renewal total was 1,732 programs, valued at $5.226 billion, in 804 localities. There were also 12 code enforcement projects, with an investment of more than $7 million; 20 demolition projects costing nearly $5 million; 157 community renewal projects, at $24 million; and 73 demonstration projects, valued in excess of $6 million.

To date, the total land area involved in urban renewal projects has been about 80,000 acres—the equivalent of all of Boston, San Francisco, and Miami. The number of new dwelling units created in urban renewal projects has been tabulated in excess of 84,000.

Among the most recent HUD programs are grants for new neighborhood centers for low-income families, providing space for social, health, and education activities—usually as part of the community action programs of the War on Poverty. Grants have been approved for 26 cities, with fund reservations coming to more than $5 million. Another related program enables federal grants to be made to help cities demolish vacant or abandoned structures regarded as public nuisances or health hazards.

## An Instance In Rochester

In the field of urban renewal and housing assistance, HUD can point to specific accomplishments in many communities across the land. For instance, the commissioner of the Urban Renewal program in Rochester, New York, reported at the end of 1966 that his relatively small metropolitan area (600,000 population) now has active programs encompassing more than 1,300 acres and involving more than 10 per cent of the city's housing, some 30,000 residents, and more than 2,000 business firms. The total net cost of the projects was estimated to be in excess of $100 million. Yet, Rochester was actually a latecomer to urban renewal and public housing. No demolition was begun until 1960. The original project has been completed on a 61-acre site where slum buildings have been replaced with a new school, an 8-acre playground, middle-income housing units, and modern light industrial buildings. The project includes more than $4 million in public improvements, and $6 million in private work.

Rochester is particularly proud of clearance activity on its 33-acre Genesee Crossroads site, in a key position along the Genesee River. Brick warehouses, wooden shanties, flophouses, and ginmills have been razed, and most of the land has been sold for private developments that will be worth more than $57 million. Included are a 300-room motor inn and two 29-story apartment buildings with 421 units.

Rochester was among the first cities to apply for a code enforcement project under Section 117 of the Housing Act of 1965.

## Other City Projects—and Problems

Although Rochester and other cities have made strong progress in urban renewal, nonetheless, HUD must face situations that indicate urban progress comes slowly—and not without anguish and infighting. Early in 1967, Secretary Weaver withdrew a commitment of $10.4 million set aside for a predominately downtown urban renewal project in Cleveland, which had never managed to get the project into being. Also, HUD refused a Cleveland application for $24 million to expand a primarily residential project involving part of the Hough area where there had been racial troubles and riots. HUD charged that Cleveland had not made a full survey of relocation housing and had lagged in building recreation centers.

On the credit side, HUD's urban renewal section could point to a Philadelphia program, in which 250 city-owned vacant lots were put to new uses as small "tot lots" or parks, and to success in Honolulu, Hawaii, which has been improving or renovating twenty-eight parks that had been allowed to become eyesores through inattention. San Pablo, California, created a new plaza named for President John F. Kennedy with the aid of a $100,127 beautification grant from HUD. In Toledo, Ohio, the first housing project designed specifically for handicapped persons in low-rent public housing has been started; the 164 living units have special facilities installed to enable handicapped and elderly persons to move about with ease and in safety.

An unusual example of cooperation among the departments of Labor, Interior, HEW, and HUD and the Office of Economic Opportunity has resulted in a program of low-rent housing in the Red Lake, White Earth, and Leech Lake Indian reservations in Minnesota. Other benefits of this program are the creation of employment opportunities on the reservations and the training of skilled construction workers.

In Guam, the Housing and Urban Renewal Authority proposed its first low-rent housing program for 250 living units that will be constructed on several sites in Agana, the capital.

The Housing Assistance Section (see Chart 5) of Assistant Secretary Hummel's responsibility has instituted a nationwide effort to reduce vacancies in low-rent housing. The goal is a national occupancy rate of 98 per cent in government-owned housing. However, the new direction in housing assistance is toward selling detached and semidetached public housing units to tenants. The first program in St. Louis involved a tenant paying $45 a month with an option to buy the 10-room rehabilitated brick house in an urban renewal area for $11,100.

If the owner is willing, the lease of a low-income unit may

include an option to purchase when and if the tenant's income exceeds public housing limits. This plan has been adopted in Benton Harbor, Michigan, with the support of local real estate leaders.

HUD's Housing Assistance Section also has taken a role in promoting neighborhood health centers. The Columbia Point public housing project in Boston has joined in a cooperative effort with the Tufts University School of Medicine and the Office of Economic Opportunity to set up a voluntary organization of residents to obtain a comprehensive program of specialty and consultative medical services and hospital care. In five months, more than 50 per cent of the project population used the services.

Finally, as part of the record, it should be noted that, in many towns and cities, HUD is using the Housing Act of 1965 to upgrade existing private housing by encouraging private real estate interests to rehabilitate residential units that have become shabby and undesirable without actually being blighted. Officials anticipate that 40,000 units will be leased over a four-year period. Requirements include rehabilitation of substandard units as a requisite for the leasing. About 25 per cent of the goal had been achieved under the annual contributions contract within a year after the program was started.

# VI

# Metropolitan Development

---

Unlike the assistant secretaryships for Mortgage Credit (FHA and FNMA) and for Renewal and Housing Assistance, the Metropolitan Development section of HUD is new, not a carryover, and essentially innovative. Metropolitan Development provides supplemental grants for programs in accordance with "sound, coordinated metropolitan planning." Included are urban planning assistance programs, planned metropolitan development incentive grants, advances for public works planning, administration of comprehensive planning requirements, metropolitan area planning coordination, mass transportation loans, grants and demonstrations; basic water and sewer grants, open space land, and urban beautification (outside central city areas), advance acquisition of land, public facilities loans, and liquidating programs.

HUD Secretary Weaver has noted that the role of Metropolitan Development concerns present and future land use as it relates to human needs within urban areas. As such, it is an expression of the concept put forth by President Johnson almost two years before HUD was created, when he told Congress: "If we are to deal successfully with the complex problems of our urban and suburban communities, we need governmental machinery designed for the 1960's, not the 1940's."

## TRANSPORTATION GRANTS

Speaking in San Francisco late in 1966, Assistant Secretary for Metropolitan Development Charles Haar said:

94

Chart 6
ASSISTANT SECRETARY FOR METROPOLITAN DEVELOPMENT

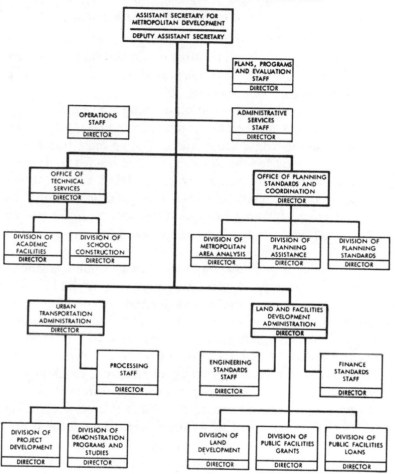

We are entering into a new era in public transportation—one in which the services you provide must receive full recognition as an essential component in the balanced, coordinated, efficient and orderly development of our cities—great and small.

He was referring to HUD programs for urban mass transportation, which are to be continued outside the even-newer-than-HUD Department of Transportation, and which are a major responsibility of his section.

On the basis of 1966 legislation, matching grants are available to state and local public agencies for two-thirds of the costs of planning, engineering, and designing mass transportation projects—and for the technical studies needed to develop an urban transit improvement program. HUD regards urban transportation and comprehensive metropolitan planning as being interrelated. The goal is good transportation for people in cities and an economic base that enables the transportation system to operate soundly.

The new legislation also provides grants to public agencies for study fellowships in mass transportation to make more trained leadership personnel available; grants to nonprofit educational institutions to assist in the establishment of training programs and comprehensive research on urban transportation; and a mandate for HUD to submit to the President and Congress early in 1968 a program of research, development, and demonstration of new systems of urban transportation.

Early in 1967, HUD announced that contracts amounting to $1.5 million had been let to begin what the *Christian Science Monitor* called a "search for an entirely new transport system in cities to fit citizens' needs of the future." Of the contracts let for studies on new kinds of equipment that may put passengers through underground tubes at hypersonic speeds, Haar said: "We hope that . . . we can come up with a design so that Congress can decide on the wisest investment of public funds."

The studies will include the use of land where mass transit equipment is used, the effect of transportation on the lives of city residents, and the coordination of transport with housing, antipollution efforts, and other elements of urban planning.

The major contract to develop the future transit report went to Stanford Research Institute of Menlo Park, California. One contract to make the accommodation study for the link between present and future public transportation went to WABCO Mass Transit Center of Westinghouse Air Brake in Pittsburgh, Pennsylvania, which will explore everything from automatic fare collection devices to electronic highway surveillance devices. Another contract, with Day & Zimmerman of Philadelphia, includes an assignment to devise means of obtaining better results from existing transportation, including relocation of streets and separation of pedestrians from vehicles. A fourth contract went to Defense Research Corporation of Santa Barbara, California, to seek a practical systems analysis of urban transportation problems.

Commenting on hoped-for results of the studies, Haar said: "Breakthroughs that can be found now can have a catalytic effect on private industry,"—which, he added, is ready to move in big ways into mass urban transportation.

Altogether, HUD had earlier approved 44 capital grants totaling nearly $157 million, 44 grants totaling $39 million for demonstration projects, and 2 capital loans aggregating more than $6 million.

HUD's basic mass transit program, as enacted in 1964, includes capital improvement and demonstration programs, each awarding grants up to two-thirds of project cost. Under it, a grant was made to provide buses, in St. Petersburg, Florida, with special hand rails for the aid of the elderly; a grant in Corpus Christi, Texas, made it possible for a bus system to remain in operation to serve low-income and older citizens in special assistance housing projects; and the Bay area of San Francisco got help for construction of its rapid rail transit system and a test of a skylounge helicopter that might take both passengers and their baggage from city centers to air terminals.

In another example of HUD support of dramatic pioneering in metropolitan transportation, a demonstration grant was given to test whether small buses circulating in the central business district of Washington, D.C., would attract riders to facilitate movement of people, reduce traffic congestion, and stimulate commercial business in the areas served.

It is interesting to note that Washington's demonstration grant was based on a plan first proposed in 1962, when Downtown Progress—a private organization dedicated to the revival of the downtown section of the capital's business area—came up with the idea of a small vehicle making low-cost trips through the central city shopping district. A study indicated a need for an electric-powered vehicle, but none could be found. After discussing the idea with thirty-six equipment manufacturers, a Downtown Progress staff member found a small West Coast firm willing to lend its "minibus" for a trial in Washington. Downtown Progress paid the freight charges that brought the vehicle to the capital. Demonstration runs were made until the District of Columbia Government, the Washington metropolitan area transit group, and the D.C. transit system cooperated to seek a HUD grant for a trial run that proved successful enough to make the minibus a regular part of D.C. transit service. Originally, the fare was 5 cents for the short rides, and use was high. When the fare was raised to 10 cents, use fell off but revenue increased. At present, eight minibuses are used in midtown, and others have been put into service to serve as shuttles between widely separated government offices around the capital city. Not long after Washington adopted the minibus, twenty-three other cities, retired citizens' communities, airports, and industrial plants were using the compact vehicles.

Obviously, public transportation can accomplish much to bring inner city and suburbs closer together—another objective of the basic HUD philosophy to make sections of the upper- and middle-income population aware of the living conditions in other, less fortunate areas.

Assistant Secretary Haar has commented in regard to future transportation and its technologies:

> Improvements in transportation may have a circular effect, stimulating new increases in the demand for transportation—and thus tending to overload even the "best" new transportation systems. Changes in transportation act as a catalyst which bring on changes in land uses—and, in fact, changes in the shape of the city. For this program (of mass transportation within HUD) coincides with and reinforces market trends. The greatest growth in employment opportunities in both industry and service during the last decade have been in the suburbs. A recent Labor Department survey showed that 62 per cent of industrial construction and 52 per cent of commercial construction in the country's metropolitan areas during the last five years were in the suburbs.

The McCone report on the riots in the Watts section of Los Angeles in 1966 indicated that the Los Angeles public transportation services were very costly in time and money to the persons using them, depriving those people of access to other parts of the sprawling metropolitan area and actually contributing to the isolation within Watts itself. It noted that some Watts residents faced financial insolvency when they overextended their credit to purchase automobiles to meet what were termed "personal needs."

Both lack of transportation facilities and the cost of using two or more separate systems without transfer arrangements have been scored for demanding an excessively large proportion of the disadvantaged consumer's budget in Los Angeles.

Considering those factors, HUD has worked with the California Transportation Agency to set up a $2.7 million demonstration project to study the relationship between the public transportation system and job and other opportunities for low-income groups in the South Central and East Los Angeles areas. Much of that money has already been designated to establish new services there.

Another demonstration grant of $482,000 went to Nashville, Tennessee, to test the impact of direct bus service linking eight separate medical centers with each other and with the central bus terminal in the downtown area of the city.

Other examples of HUD's efforts in the field of public transportation can be found in Towson, Maryland, where a $53,350 grant is helping to test the economic feasibility and desirability of providing a suburban "town center" and its surrounding low-density, moderately high-income residential areas with express bus service to the downtown shopping and employment areas—using modern, air-conditioned equipment operating over controlled access freeways at speeds comparable to that achieved by private cars. Also, in Chesapeake, Virginia, a $241,288 HUD grant is being utilized to determine whether the residents of that growing Norfolk-Portsmouth area can use mass transportation to the labor center, if the service is frequent, reasonable in cost, and available when new residents move into the community.

A 1966 amendment to the Urban Mass Transportation Act enabled HUD to grant $369,334 to the Atlanta (Georgia) Metropolitan Rapid Transit Authority to finance two-thirds of the cost of the technical studies needed to submit a coordinated rapid-transit-system improvement proposal to Atlanta voters in a bond election. The Transit Authority planned to supplement the HUD grant with $184,667. Assistant Secretary Haar commented on the Atlanta grant:

> We do not regard a transportation system as something that can be superimposed on a city after all else is planned or built. It is our firm conviction that transportation systems are a vital component of metropolitan development and effective metropolitan planning must bring the people operating the system into the planning process at an early state of deliberations.

## URBAN PLANNING ASSISTANCE

In the field of urban planning assistance, HUD's metropolitan program is designed to foster good community, area, regional, and statewide planning. Popularly called the Section

701 program, it has antecedents dating back to that portion of the Housing Act of 1954, as amended. Federal grants of two-thirds of the cost of the work of comprehensive planning for public facilities and transportation and long-term fiscal structures are made against local contributions of one-third of the cost. In some instances, the federal contribution can be as much as 75 per cent. Cities and other municipalities with less than 50,000 population and counties and Indian reservations are eligible too.

Metropolitan Development's Assistant Secretary Haar has insisted that planning holds the key to the future of all cities, large or small.

> We know we are going to have to build an urban America in the next 35 years equal to all we have built since Jamestown. The question now is, what is it going to look like: And how can all citizens be given more of a choice of where and how they want to live? The initiative is with the local area to develop its own plan—a plan that is consistent with other over-all planning, involving the locality.

In recent years, urban planning has increased throughout the United States, with nearly one-fifth of the grants approved in 1966. One of the smallest localities of the 2,700 participating is Saxman, Alaska, an Indian village of 153 inhabitants. A $3,000 grant was made for Saxman to study its problems of land ownership, housing, utilities, and general blight and also to plan for better land use, transportation, town beautification, and local government.

## Metropolitan Development Grants

Planned metropolitan development also is part of the HUD portfolio of metropolitan programs. New legislation enables the HUD Secretary to authorize supplemental grants to state and local public bodies and agencies for up to 20 per cent of the cost of projects receiving aid under other federal programs in metropolitan areas where development is being carried out in accordance with local planning. The supplemental grant is designed as an incentive for coordinated metropolitan development. Administration of these grants is divided, according to the project, by HUD, HEW, Interior, and Commerce, and the Federal Aviation Administration. A basic stipulation is that the total federal contribution to a project may not exceed 80 per cent.

Since June 30, 1967, all applications for federal assistance for projects in which supplemental grants can be provided must be submitted to a metropolitan or regional planning agency for review. The HUD Secretary is authorized to call on other federal agencies to cooperate in insuring that all federal programs related to metropolitan development be carried out in a coordinated manner. If local officials request, the HUD Secretary may appoint a metropolitan expediter for the area.

## PUBLIC WORKS

Basic water and sewer facilities are regarded as growth needs. Some communities need these facilities in order to provide more homes or to attract new industry. HUD has been authorized to help meet the needs of small communities by providing the long-term loans for the construction of needed public works. Private investors must get the first chance to provide needed credit, and HUD buys the bonds only when private investors do not offer to take them at the same or better rates.

The public facility loan program is the successor to a series of public works programs that were initiated in the 1930's in order to stimulate employment and help get the nation out of Depression doldrums. The public facility loan program for basic water and sewer facilities, utility systems, hospitals, community buildings, city streets, and airport improvements affected 1,058 projects for $400 million in loans in 46 states and 1 territory during the first year of Metropolitan Development programs. During the same period, under a separate grant program, basic water and sewer facilities involved 220 projects for a total of $115 million in 38 states and 1 territory.

One of those basic sewer and water facilities programs went to Kinloch, Missouri, a community of 6,500, with a reported 98 per cent of the families at a poverty level. The $684,000 sewer grant was made to provide a waste collection system to combat pollution. The sewer installation is expected to reduce public health problems and also stimulate industrial development and economic growth in the town near St. Louis.

Still another related program involved planning assistance for individual public works that help communities to deal with their total needs. Interest-free advances of funds can be made to public agencies to cover the cost of plan preparation. Repayment is required when construction begins. Grants for 2,658 projects involving $118 million were made through 1966 in all of the 50 states and 3 territories. One of those advances for public works planning was designated for a new high school to serve educational needs in Worden, Yellowstone County, Montana, where the junior high school was built in 1913 and the senior high school in 1939. When the new senior high school becomes available, the present senior high structure will be used for junior high students. This community got $8,735 for preliminary planning of the proposed school, estimated to cost nearly $500,000.

## Open Land

Another HUD interest concerns its financing aid to help localities acquire and develop open land for parks. and recreation. The outdoor resource must be within an urban area and within easy commuting distance for every citizen. HUD has assisted 277 localities to purchase 41,000 acres of open land in 35 states, and its contribution amounted to $41 million. HUD's open-space program can be used to help a city such as Fresno, California, combine flood control, recreation, and water conservation in a single project. Under this unique Fresno program, land used for parks and recreation during the dry months serves to refill Fresno's underground water supply during the rainy season. For it, HUD awarded $82,000 to aid in the acquisition of 66 acres of land. Sites are used for recreation 10 months of the year, but serve as storm water retention basins during the rainy season, thus utilizing as much as possible Fresno's meager 11 annual inches of rain.

## URBAN BEAUTIFICATION

A program akin to the open lands idea was fashioned to assist cities, towns, and localities in carrying out urban beautification programs. Parks and related recreation uses are part of the general objectives that include conservation, scenic areas, and preservation of historic places. Urban beautification and improvement includes street landscaping, park improvements, tree planting, and upgrading of malls and squares.

Philadelphia, as an example, is creating 250 vest-pocket parks in congested neighborhoods where recreation and green space have been missing. Transformed from publicly owned vacant lots, these tiny parks are special features of a citywide program that will involve beautification of several major plazas with fountains, walkways, and plantings, as well as other tree plantings and general landscaping work. HUD's $1,005,125 grant to Philadelphia, under the urban beautification program, will cover half of the $2,009,250 eligible increased annual cost represented in the $2,684,706 the city plans to spend on a beautification effort. Nationally, Metropolitan Development programs accounted for urban beautification projects in 63 cities and towns for a total of almost $10 million, with 17 different states participating.

Federal assistance has been increased to 50 per cent to help public agencies acquire and preserve urban lands having value for park, recreation, scenic, or historic purposes. (Similar 50 per cent assistance also is available to assist in developing lands acquired under the open-space land program.) A grant for urban beautification can range up to 50 per cent of the cost of the project. However, grants up to 90 per cent are authorized to carry out projects of special value for the demonstration of new and improved methods and materials for urban beautification.

An areawide development program is required, and beautification activities must have long-term benefits to the area.

An example of combined open-space land and beautification grants was a $10, 680 project that enabled Milton, Massachusetts, to help preserve the historic roadbed of the horse-drawn railway that carried the blocks for the Bunker Hill Monument. The site also was developed for park, recreation, and conservation uses.

## ADVANCE ACQUISITION LOANS

Increasing land costs have made the advance acquisition of sites for public facilities burdensome for small communities. In 1965, the federal government established a new grant program designed to aid these localities to make timely and well-planned purchases of sites. Under it, today, HUD will pay the reasonable interest charges on a loan obtained to purchase land up to five years in advance of proposed construction of public facilities. Those facilities must be designed to contribute to the economy, efficiency, and planned development of the area.

Any public body with legal authority to acquire and finance land for future construction of public facilities may apply for grant assistance. Cities, towns, village, townships, counties, Indian tribes, special districts, and combinations of any of these are eligible. As is the case with most HUD programs, the first step is to obtain necessary forms and information from the HUD regional office serving the area.

## LONG-RANGE OBJECTIVES

The foregoing examples of projects in being are illustrative of the HUD effort in transportation and other fields. They must all be reckoned as innovations that will influence the future development of metropolitan areas. Modernizing transit lines and preserving open land adjacent to cities, as well as improvements of every kind in the metropolitan areas themselves, will affect the lives of all city dwellers.

One of the final acts of the 1966 Congress was to authorize comprehensive planning incentives in the form of supplementary grants for federally assisted programs that have a direct bearing on present and future land use in relation to human needs. Metropolitan areas and cities have launched more than 1,200 community development programs and projects with about $300 million in HUD support as well as technical assistance.

These projects were funded in part with advances, loans, and grants from HUD's Metropolitan Development Office. The projects range from libraries to transit systems and from hospitals and community centers to city streets and open space land and parks.

Altogether, the federal and HUD emphasis is being strengthened to provide, encourage, and demand incentives for more areawide planning coordination. More than 300 such programs were undertaken in 1966.

The Metropolitan Development role of HUD is based on long-range objectives for both large cities and small towns— making grants for the projects that contribute to better living for all people as part of municipal, county, regional, or state growth. A look at the HUD metropolitan grants for one week in 1966 showed a wide range of public works planning programs as seed money for larger projects: The list included $2,000 to little Roy, Washington, to finance planning of a municipal water distribution system to cost a total of $159,000; the scores of sewerage facilities programs include a grant of $14,050 to finance planning of municipal sewerage facilities in Whitefield, New Hampshire, that will cost the town a total of $721,550; and another unglamorous but highly important project involved a grant of $3,775 to Leoti, Kansas, to finance planning of storm drainage improvements to cost a total of $345,000.

Before the Community Facilities Administration lost its name in the HUD organization, its programs—now one part of Metropolitan Development—had helped nearly 4,000 communities with projects that totaled $94 million in interest-free advances, which, essentially, constitute a revolving fund from which a basic federal financial contribution enables funds to go out to help one town do something in municipal construction and then pay back the money to be put into use again to help another community get started on a similar project. These projects continue to benefit the country. And now, many new ones are being added.

Not one of HUD's headline-grabbing activities, the Metropolitan Development programs are, nevertheless, highly regarded throughout the United States. Without them, many towns and cities could not get started on transport, water, sewer, and other "housekeeping" construction necessary for community survival.

# VII

## Demonstrations and Intergovernmental Relations: The "Model Cities" Program

The Demonstration Cities and Metropolitan Development Act of 1966 authorized the HUD Secretary to provide grants and technical assistance to help communities plan, develop, and carry out comprehensive city demonstration programs for the rebuilding or restoring of entire sections or neighborhoods of slums and blighted areas. The "Model Cities" program, as it is commonly called, was set up to operate on the basis of assistance for planning and developing local programs and then, after July 1, 1967, to provide assistance to carry out these programs. (For full text, see Appendix I.)

The first deadline for applications from cities and metropolitan counties for funds under the Act was May 1, 1967. On that date, 192 applications from urban areas in 47 states had been received. Cities and towns of every size, from Alviso, California, with a population of 1,174, to New York City, with a population exceeding 8 million, were represented.

Within HUD, the responsibility for processing these applications, and for all the extensive activities that fall within the ken of the Demonstration Cities legislation, is centered in the Office of Demonstrations and Intergovernmental Relations, headed by an assistant secretary.

Shortly after the Act was signed into law on November 3, 1966, HUD Secretary Weaver said that its "emphasis is on innovation." Addressing officials of New Jersey cities and municipalities, he stressed that rearranged and expanded old programs would not do the job of reaching alienated slum dwellers. He urged new approaches and new methods to speed up building or rebuilding.

Outside of HUD, the Act was regarded as a sort of companion or follow-up to the creation of HUD itself, with the object of helping cities make their renewal projects contribute to educational and employment opportunities and health, as well as housing, for residents. Spokesmen for HUD pointed out that the model neighborhood program would be able to deliver a "total attack" on social and physical problems in slum and blighted areas, and they stressed the importance of comprehensiveness, coordination, and, again, innovation in the effort.

About ten weeks after the model cities legislation was signed into law, both Secretary Weaver and Assistant Secretary for Demonstrations and Intergovernmental Relations H. Ralph Taylor announced that the program was "in business"—with $11 million to spend in the fiscal year ending June 30, 1967. Additional funds authorized by Congress included $12 million in planning grants, $400 million in supplementary funds for the year ending June 30, 1968, and $250 million in grants for urban renewal projects in model city neighborhoods. Early interest indicated that applications would exceed available funds to develop comprehensive programs to revitalize inner city neighborhood areas. Secretary Weaver said that applications by cities would be prepared in accordance with standards published in the 57-page *Program Guide to Model Neighborhoods and Demonstration Cities.**

MODEL CITIES

In particular, HUD expected that participants in the Model Cities program would:

Search for new paths to the local solution of local problems;

Link projects and activities designed to develop human resources with those for improving physical environment;

* Available for 55 cents from the Superintendent of Documents, U.S. Government Printing Office, Washington, D.C. 20301.

Provide new and improved housing and community facilities for health, education, transportation, employment, shopping, recreation, and culture;

Provide a substantial increase in the supply of standard housing for low- and moderate-income families;

Open up opportunities for involvement of citizens in the neighborhoods and the city as a whole in planning and carrying out the major activities;

Encourage private initiative and enterprise of individual home owners, contractors, and builders and involve business and financial interests in carrying out a program in which private enterprise can prosper in meeting the needs of the residents, whether through construction or the new jobs generated by new commercial and industrial enterprises.

Areas eligible for participation in the model or demonstration program were to be selected by the locality on the basis of serious housing and environmental deficiencies, and high concentration of poverty, unemployment, ill health, and lack of education. It was also stipulated that the area should be large enough to remove blight and decay in entire neighborhoods—roughly about 10 per cent of a city's total population.

Intrinsically, the Demonstration Cities Act has taken up many of the principles of the Economic Opportunities Act in enlarging the federal commitment to social action at the local level. Because of the enormous potential, the cost figures for model city projects are recognized as merely the first installment on the billions of dollars that may be required in the next ten years. The most expensive part of the program probably will be providing the financial encouragement necessary for cities to perform major surgery and therapy in such areas as Harlem in New York and Watts in Los Angeles.

The basic program standards specified by HUD include:

An attack on blighted housing—an expanded supply of standard housing is a major objective—and impact on physical and social problems of a neighborhood;

A contribution to the sound development of the total city;

Progress in reducing social and educational disadvantages

and relieving illness, underemployment, and enforced idleness;

Widespread citizen participation;

Creation of opportunities for training and employing area residents;

Maximum opportunity in housing choices for all citizens;

Adequate public and commercial facilities for residents;

Easier access between neighborhoods and centers of employment;

High standards of design;

Preservation of natural and historic sites and distinctive neighborhood characteristics;

Maximum use of new technology and cost reduction aids.

One provision of the Act stipulated that assistance be given to cities of all sizes. For small cities that do not have all of the problems or conditions delineated for eligibility, the HUD demonstration program may be tailored for planning and grant assistance by including social services and activities appropriate to the size and circumstances. Also, Congress directed HUD to take into consideration in its assessments and decisions that smaller cities do not have full staffs of planning experts and technicians.

Cities will be granted up to 80 per cent of the cost of planning their demonstration projects, and they will be expected to use existing federal aids directed against slum blight. Those existing programs include many already established HUD activities in urban renewal, public housing, housing for the elderly, and FHA mortgage insurance programs for low- and moderate-income housing—plus the newer rent supplement program administered under FHA. In addition, there can be correlation with other government programs in the fields of welfare, health, Medicare, and federal grants for transit, highways, and schools.

The participating cities are expected to use their own—or state or private—resources to provide 20 per cent or more of the total cost of the comprehensive planning for model city projects. Initially, assistance is provided to plan and develop demonstration programs; later, other assistance is to be provided to carry out the planned programs. Most of the comprehensive planning is done under the amended "701 Program," which has enabled over-all, multijurisdiction comprehensive planning agencies to be set up in more than 170 areas.

Commenting on this phase of model city planning activity, Assistant Secretary Taylor told the National Association of Housing and Redevelopment Officials:

> The financing of the program is not as complicated as it may appear. Let us assume that a city proposes in its demonstration program an array of federally assisted programs that involve $20 million in nonfederal contributions. These might include some neighborhood parks, tot lots, green areas, an urban renewal project, a health services program, a neighborhood center, an adult education program, a manpower and job-training program —whatever the city thinks it would take to accomplish a significant improvement in the neighborhood and the quality of the lives of its people.
>
> In this hypothetical case, the $20 million in local share of these programs will generate, under the financing formula, supplemental funds of 80 per cent of this amount, or $16 million. Now the great new thrust in this program lies in the fact that these supplemental funds do not have to be "earmarked" for any one specific project or activity. They may be used for any project or activity included as part of the demonstration program. A city may, for example, want to use this money for stepped-up garbage collection, a police–community relations program, or supplemental health services, or experiments in housing rehabilitation and ownership patterns or—well, I could go on and on, and so could you.
>
> In the hypothetical case I have just cited, the federal share of the total program might—if we take a two-to-one ratio such as the one in the urban renewal and neighborhood centers— come to $40 million. Add that to the $20 million of local contributions and the $16 million in the 80 per cent supplemental funds, and you have a total of $76 million.

HUD's widespread interest in community level action has already been demonstrated in little Douglas, Georgia, where slums have been virtually eliminated. HUD published a report, "Looking Over Douglas' Shoulder," updating an earlier study (made in 1957) to show that an approved workable program is a prerequisite for certain federal housing and urban renewal aids. It was pointed out that the town achieved its objectives in a master plan by shifting the location of a facility or changing a method to suit circumstances. H. Ralph Taylor, HUD Assistant Secretary for Demonstrations and Intergovernmental Relations, said that Douglas had worked out a program oriented to human needs to relocate, in decent housing, marginal-income families and those displaced by public projects.

Listed among the community's achievements were completion of two urban renewal projects and a third under way; replacement of 200 substandard structures with 130 units of low-rent public housing, 40 conventionally financed homes, and 35 middle-income homes financed under FHA's 221(d)(3) program; and a 185 per cent increase in total employment. Also completed were three recreational areas, a new city hall, a nursing home for the elderly, two new elementary schools, and a civic center. Major improvements were made in the traffic system and in downtown parking. Authorized by Section 314 of the Housing Act of 1954, the Douglas urban renewal demonstration grant program was eligible for up to two-thirds of the cost of work aimed at improving urban renewal methods and techniques.

To be part of such a planning program, the area must give HUD a list of its problems, be classed as a metropolitan region, and conform to the established HUD pattern. An outstanding example of the kind of planning necessary for model city activity is Philadelphia, where HUD aid was asked for the planning of a program expected to cost more than $235 million over a five-year span. A 350-page proposal was submitted that sought, initially, a $750,000 HUD grant that would enable Philadelphia to begin at least six months of intensive planning for its objectives. Meeting those objectives was estimated to cost about $25 million in the first year, during which the target area would be the northwest and north central sectors of the city, where activity would include rehabilitation of homes, setting up employment centers, provid-

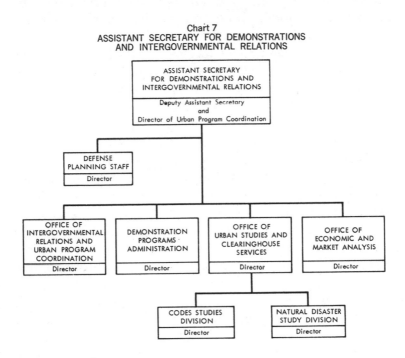

Chart 7
ASSISTANT SECRETARY FOR DEMONSTRATIONS
AND INTERGOVERNMENTAL RELATIONS

ing better police protection, and other civic and environmental improvements in the neighborhoods.

Philadelphia's city development coordinator drafted the proposal and said it would be coordinated with urban renewal projects already under way or planned. He also noted that a fifteen-man policy group would serve in an advisory capacity. This proposal follows the lines suggested by Assistant Secretary Taylor.

DEMONSTRATION PROJECTS

Two distinct functions fall under the "Demonstrations" responsibility. In addition to model or demonstration cities, the assistant secretary also oversees other specific demonstration projects.

An example of a specific demonstration project is the HUD-sponsored, $136,000 report called "Neighborhood Conservation in New York City." This report describes a coordinated attempt by public and private agencies to define and attack both physical and social deficiencies in seven New York City neighborhoods from 1955 to 1963. The program sought to develop alternatives to mass demolition and relocation in areas where urban renewal was not planned.

Another example came soon after the Demonstrations legislation was enacted, with approval of a grant of $519,493 to the Metropolitan Washington (D.C.) Council of Governments—the regional planning agency for the metropolitan area including the nation's capital. At about the same time, but under a grant made possible by the prior Housing Act of 1961, as amended, Secretary Weaver announced approval of a $200,000 project to demonstrate the development of low-income housing in a mix with existing middle- and high-income housing in the new town of Reston, Virginia, about twenty-three miles northwest of Washington, D.C. This project was set up to show how new technology, in design, architecture, production, and planning can be used. The grant covered cost of the architectural planning, social analysis, design and production of prototype homes, and an evaluation of the demonstration, which will test factory-fabricated steel houses of 1,200 square feet with two, three, and four bedrooms. Produced off site and then assembled at Reston, the structures include townhouse clusters and garden apartments.

OTHER RESPONSIBILITIES

Among other responsibilities of HUD's Office for Demonstrations and Intergovernmental Relations are:

Housing research and urban studies programs authorized by the Housing acts of 1948 and 1956, as amended;

Defense planning and emergency preparedness functions and the Department's natural disaster relief activities and representation at the Office of Emergency Planning's Resources Evaluation Center;

Development of policies, standards, and procedures for and

supervision of the conduct of comprehensive market analyses;

Comprehensive national studies and analyses of developments, trends, and problems in the areas of housing markets and the needs of the capital mortgage market and related economic analyses;

Studies of housing and building codes, tax policies, and development of standards authorized in the Housing Act of 1965;

Study of alternative programs for providing financial assistance in connection with natural disasters under the Southeast Hurricane Disaster Relief Act of 1965;

Technical assistance, studies, and publications relating to open-space land and urban beautification under Section 708 of the Housing Act of 1961, as amended;

Urban renewal demonstration programs under Section 314 of the Housing Act of 1954, as amended.

## THE INTERGOVERNMENTAL RELATIONS PORTFOLIO

The assistant secretary for Demonstrations and Intergovernmental Relations must, of necessity, be involved in a great deal of agency activity at the state and local levels; hence, the second part of his title.

To illustrate, HUD is a sponsor of a Lighthouse Neighborhood Center Project, in Washington, D.C., along with the Department of Labor, the Department of Health, Education, and Welfare, the Office of Economic Opportunity, and the Bureau of the Budget. Other cities invited to take part in the project to show the impact of providing broad public and private services to needy people at the neighborhood level are Boston, New York, Philadelphia, Louisville, Jacksonville, Chattanooga, Chicago, Detroit, Cincinnati, Minneapolis, St. Paul, Dallas, and Oakland. Assistant Secretary Taylor said the experiment would provide experience for using the model city legislation effectively, noting that federal effort must be coordinated with varied groups and agencies in cities themselves. HUD can provide some money to build and rehabilitate neighborhood centers, but operating money must come from agencies working with HUD or from existing federal grant programs.

In his governmental role, the assistant secretary is seeking to develop effective working relationships with other federal agencies that have basic interests in community development programs and to find effective ways of providing a source of information and advice on the problems that arise in the administration of federal programs requiring cooperation among federal, state, and local governments in their own development of arrangements to discharge their metropolitan obligations efficiently.

Long experience in local urban renewal projects enabled Assistant Secretary Taylor to bring an understanding of intergovernmental procedures to his HUD post. Working closely with Secretary Weaver on all aspects of the Department's relations with other government agencies in Washington and elsewhere, Taylor regarded the intergovernmental side of his office as sufficiently important to warrant bringing into it a career federal employee, Norman Beckman, who had had experience in the Bureau of the Budget, and with the Advisory Commission on Intergovernmental Relations. Beckman was named director of the Office of Intergovernmental Relations and Urban Program Coordination. He has set up a staff of fifteen to establish good working relationships with other federal agencies that have coinciding interests and, also, to assist and encourage state, county, and local governments to work together on areawide objectives when HUD and other federal fund programs are involved.

"We have a significant, difficult-to-define job to do in intergovernmental relations," Beckman has commented. "We try to keep our feet on the ground by recalling from time to time (Deputy Secretary of HUD) Bob Wood's definition of Washington as ten square miles surrounded by reality. We must deal with both."

HUD's particularly keen interest in intergovernmental relations stems from the nature of its key programs and from a Presidential behest to the HUD Secretary to lead a national effort for increased cooperation within the so-called creative federalism.

A primary responsibility for harnessing government agencies for the attack on problems of the cities was assigned to the HUD Secretary by President Johnson in August, 1966, when an executive order gave the HUD Secretary authority to call meetings of all federal executives handling programs affecting urban areas.

Shortly thereafter, a Senate subcommittee headed by Senator Abraham Ribicoff, held hearings at which Secretary Weaver was scolded by Ribicoff and Senator Robert Kennedy for perpetuating a delusion that the nation is attacking the housing ills of its slums, where violence has flared. Both senators waded into Secretary Weaver for lack of aggressiveness in coordinating programs to aid slum dwellers. (The criticism even went to the extent that Ribicoff said that Weaver should have sought to shift an urban rat control program from the Interior Department's Fish and Wildlife Service to HUD. Ribicoff said that rats killed or maimed 14,000 slum dwellers in one year, 1965, but that only $27,500 had been allocated for federal rat control in urban areas.) Secretary Weaver insisted that enactment of the demonstration or model cities program would spur a coordinated federal effort to rebuild slum areas. When faced with the criticism that the "job is not being done," Weaver reported that lack of local response had been a cause, thus prompting Senator Kennedy to say: "Arguments over who should do the job—the federal government, the states, the cities—won't solve problems. We're not using the kind of imagination we used on the Marshall Plan . . . and the people in the cities and the slums are suffering."

A significant step toward the fundamental improvement of the system of federalism was taken late in 1966 when President Johnson issued a memorandum to heads of departments and agencies. The President said:

The basis of creative federalism is cooperation. If Federal assistance programs to state and local governments are to achieve their goals, more is needed than money alone. . . . To the fullest practical extent, I want you to take steps to afford representatives of the chief executives of state and local government the opportunity to advise and consult in the development and execution of programs which directly affect the conduct of state and local affairs. . . . Our objective is to make certain that vital new Federal assistance programs are made workable at the point of impact.

HUD Secretary Weaver took note of his responsibility in this area in testimony given to the Senate Subcommittee on Intergovernmental Relations when he said that HUD had set up organizational machinery through the assistant HUD secretary for Demonstrations and Intergovernmental Relations and the director of Intergovernmental Relations and Urban Program Coordination to insure working relationships relating to HUD goals. He said then:

More important than any major additional Executive Office staff mechanism for coordination is agreement and action by the departments and agencies in our common mission of meeting urban needs. We believe this Department, with its seat in the Cabinet, with congressional and Presidential directives, with major grant programs, and with a broad constituency of urban interest, is now in a better position than ever before to make this mission a meaningful part of policymaking and administrative practice.

The Secretary indicated that his office already had received a wide range of inquiries and requests from within and without HUD seeking to begin a "dialogue on common interests." He specified that HUD officials had established rapport with their counterparts in the Office of Economic Opportunity and in the Department of Health, Education, and Welfare.

Basic to dialogues on intergovernmental relations are the increasing federal grant-in-aid programs, of which HUD has about twenty expanded grants programs and a total of more than sixty grant, loan, and loan insurance programs.

Federal officials are aware that grant programs are many and that they have both related and unrelated objectives. Requirements and procedures vary. Also recognized are the problems of the timing of federal aid and occasional insensitivity to local purposes. Of course, uncertainty as to the availability of funds is common to all federal projects.

Secretary Weaver cited HUD's most perplexing challenge as the increasing concentration of social and economic problems in the old sections of large cities. One of the other major problems, according to Weaver, is that the United States lacks metropolitan leadership responsive to areawide problems and responsible to an areawide electorate.

Weaver said that state and local governments provide other built-in hindrances to carrying out national goals. "Some of the fifteen states having referendum requirements for public housing and urban renewal are weighted against approval." But he added that the model cities program provides HUD an opportunity to make grants for research on needed revisions of state laws affecting local governments.

At the HUD Conference of Governors' Representatives held early in 1967 at Airlie House, Warrenton, Virginia, near Washington, called by Secretary Weaver in the interest of improving HUD-state relations in meeting common urban problems, Senator Edmund Muskie, who heads the Subcommittee on Intergovernmental Relations of the Senate Committee on Government Operations, opened the conference with this statement:

> In a sense, your endeavor is a new venture in intergovernmental cooperation. In another sense, your task is as old as our Republic, that is, making our democratic government work as an instrument of freedom and opportunity. The underlying assumption of the Founding Fathers was that our society would achieve fulfillment as society made it possible for the individual to achieve fulfillment. Today, then, when we speak of the Great

*[handwritten margin note: p. 121 — Reaction to the open housing stipulation on funds.]*

...ation of the work which

...7, 70 per cent of all ...grams would be dis-

## ...ISLATION

...the model cities legisla-... /er has said that it

...l agencies to make avail-...e of federal program aids, ...he problems, rather than ...rogram basis. It requires, ...d the preparation of pro-...olvement of the agencies, ...ommunity.

...o "set the national goals ...ility."

...ot unexpectedly, strong. ...er 31, 1966) comment-...ontrol over cities, noted ...fect that a city or suburb ...ents from one district to another in order to qualify for the new type of aid." But, it went on, "there is a requirement for 'open housing' in neighborhoods that are rebuilt with this money."

Opposition to open housing in some areas has been extreme.

One of the major conclusions reached by HUD officials has been simply stated: The problems of cities are too complex to be solved by bulldozer action. Therefore, broad programs are being planned and effected. But first, according to HUD doctrine, each metropolitan area must know itself, and be able to tote up its budget on the basis of all local jurisdictions, plus state, federal, and private contributions, to do a thorough project planning job.

A HUD official has said that the model city program seeks to integrate disparate city functions, from welfare to transportation, in order to overcome social as well as physical roadblocks on the path to a decent living standard for all people. "We have found that services provided citywide just were not accessible to the poor," he said. Another pointed out that Congress must be expected to provide much more than the original $900 million, if the new model city and demonstration programs are to be fulfilled. And because the money supply is always inadequate at all levels of metropolitan project planning, HUD officials are encouraging communities to innovate in every possible way.

The 1966 housing law gave the HUD Secretary authority to appoint a metropolitan expediter for an area on the request of local officials of the central city area, after consultation with local government authorities.

The role of the expediter is to provide information, data, and assistance to local authorities and others in the area in regard to programs and activities conducted there by HUD. In addition, he has the obligation to assist and work with other public and private activities within the area in relation to common problems and programs.

Also, the Secretary is authorized to make matching grants to states to help the financing of programs to provide small communities (less than 100,000) with information and data on urban needs and assistance activities, and technical assistance for the solution of local problems.

Other kinds of help can come from HUD's older housing and financing machinery. For example, although not part of the model city side of HUD, new programs in FHA and FNMA are expected to be meshed into its workings. This is true of the new FHA-insured mortgages to enable low-income families to purchase homes at below-market interest rates and the recent authorization to FNMA to make FHA-insured advances during construction on FHA-insured mortgaged properties to stimulate more low-income housing.

Among housing professionals, the model city legislation so far has failed to stir up great enthusiasm in regard to its possible effects on the dollar-conscious residential-construction and mortgage-lending industries. One comment was that the program "might sound good and read well, but it still requires money to make it move and operate." As if in answer to this criticism, Assistant Secretary Taylor told a group in New Haven, Connecticut, on November 22, 1966, that

> The provision of housing for lower-income families is a matter of highest priority. . . . There never has been a federal program of this scope, magnitude and opportunity. Every city has a vast subterranean stream of creativity that has never been tapped. Under the model cities program it can be tapped and channeled into areas of greatest usefulness for improving the quality of urban life.

A few months later, he told a group in Florida that

> We are seeking primarily residential rehabilitation and redevelopment in model city neighborhoods. . . . What we are seeing here (in housing experiments) is a most sophisticated involvement and cooperation between government and private enterprise —a working relationship that, I am sure, would have caused the social reformers of the nineteenth century to blanch.

HUD officials stress that earlier programs of urban aid centered on specific problems while ignoring other urban ills that contributed to citizen despair and despondency. In this respect, Secretary Weaver has clarified his conception of the model cities program by saying that it could help in solving many local problems, including the causes of the urban ghetto.

"This is the most urgent problem—to bring about a rapid and tangible improvement in the quality of life for all who are impacted in these ghettos," he said.

# VIII

## HUD, Congress, and the Home Builders

All top-level members of the HUD Secretary's team are strongly conscious of their responsibility to achieve better intergovernmental relations on the state and local scenes and to maintain good liaison with Congressional committees. Similarly, all of HUD's upper-echelon political appointees and top-grade civil servants can be assumed to have learned long ago the survival requisite in maintaining satisfactory—or at least, the best possible—relations with all members of both the Senate and the House and, particularly, with the powerful party leaders on both sides of the legislative aisle. HUD's existence, as the discussion in Chapter II emphasized, is directly attributable to crucial vote switches on Capitol Hill. Many of the men who cast the votes that brought HUD into being are still in office. And, of course, each session of Congress finds a new legislative proposal, even a combination of bills, advanced in behalf of housing and urban development—some bills with features not to HUD's liking. A government department or agency can never have too many friends in Congress. HUD also needs friends in the vast home-building industry, which has strong lobbies on the Hill.

Naturally, HUD's chief impression on the Congress and on the industry is made by the Secretary himself. Observers have noted that Secretary Weaver's ability to project himself and the Department has registered with both audiences. Without being a backslapper or a wily string-puller, Weaver has managed to use his own personality, experience, and erudition to satisfy most members of the Senate and the House and the housing industry that he and his staff are operating effectively in fields where problems are far more plentiful than pat answers.

## LEGISLATIVE LIAISON

In order to expedite its relations with Congress, HUD has set up a legislative liaison staff, headed by Washington veteran Sidney Spector, to keep in close touch with members of key Senate and House committees and to be ready to act or react whenever any member of Congress has a question, a problem, or a request.

Much of the credit, on the government agency side, for the creation of HUD has been rightfully directed to the legislative liaison talents of Milton Semer, former HHFA general counsel, and Charles M. Smith, liaison leader. "We had swinging doors between our offices in those demanding days of 1965 when the HUD bill was pregnant on Capitol Hill," recalled Smith, now staff director of the Senate Subcommittee on Intergovernmental Relations.

Both Semer and Smith have pointed out, too, that they had assistance from liaison aides from the then established housing agencies. "And from the outside, we had the top-notch and unstinting support of the National Association of Home Builders —certainly the most effective and helpful force for the HUD legislative success to be obtained outside of government," said Smith.

HUD liaison veterans accept that it is extremely difficult to maintain supporting groups in the House and Senate for everything relating to housing. "The supporters vary with particular bills being considered," according to Smith, who has noted that one senator may be extremely interested in an urban renewal measure, but cool to anything involving public housing. Always, upcoming legislation must be explained to the legislators on the basis of how it will affect their home areas.

In dealing with Congress, HUD liaison men have learned to avoid a "big city" tag on specific proposals and to identify with the political interests of individual members. "You cannot depend on massive last-minute pressures to get the votes," Smith has said. "It is more important to do your work effectively during the session by explaining what the visible results are for the legislator's constituency back home and how those results will reflect on the individual Senator or Representative."

Congressional liaison by private enterprise can be practiced as an art form involving wining and dining. Not so with the normal Congressional relationships of federal departments, such as HUD. The large agencies with funding requirements generally base their success in winning friends on the Hill substantially on ability to furnish data to support causes, plus an ability to react favorably to the political requests of officeholders. And very pertinent, too, of course, is the ability of the department's or agency's liaison staff to work harmoniously with the strong liaison representation from the White House.

In presenting new legislative proposals to Congress, HUD and other departments depend on the expertise of their general counsels. HUD's new general counsel, succeeding Milton Semer, is young Thomas McGrath, of Margate, New Jersey, who was returned to Washington in the sensitive HUD post not long after being defeated for re-election to a House seat. Although it has long been a political custom for Presidents to give federal appointments to defeated members of Congress, it is considered noteworthy that McGrath turned up in the HUD structure as a general counsel whose Capitol Hill background would serve him well.

During the years when new housing starts were rolling along at a strong pace and mortgage money was plentiful, much of the Capitol Hill interest in HHFA and FHA was focused on how well things were going. However, a change in the national

financing pattern, with high interest rates and restricted lending for housing, occurred in the mid-1960's and brought
broader discussions on the Hill.

Almost as soon as he was seated in the Senate, Republican
Charles H. Percy obtained a place on the housing subcommittee and began to build himself a reputation as a Republican
spokesman on urban affairs, indicating his own and his party's
new concern in attracting urban voters. Percy proposed a
"National Housing Ownership Foundation," which would
foster rehabilitation of slum dwellings by using funds from tax-
exempt bonds backed by the government. His proposal envisioned helping the poor to rebuild their own homes or to
acquire possession through low-interest mortgages.

On the House side of the Capitol in 1967, HUD found itself facing a Ninetieth Congress that included a reorganized
House appropriations subcommittee handling fund allocations
for independent offices and the new HUD. It was noted by
observers that the makeup of the subcommittee might be cool
to Administration spending programs generally and possibly
unsympathetic to new HUD programs, because six of its ten
members were from towns whose population is less than
30,000. Chairman Joe L. Evins, Democrat of Tennessee, from
Smithville (less than 3,000 population), said that it was unfair
to prejudge his subcommittee on the basis of small-town roots.
He insisted that the fate of new and old HUD programs in
obtaining financing would depend on how effectively the HUD
officials were able to present their cases.

## CASE STUDY OF A LOBBY

One of the many groups that made policy statements and
actively engaged in the legislative liaison connected with passage of the HUD bill (see also Chapter II), the National Association of Home Builders has for years been regarded as the
spokesman of the vast home-building industry and also as a
respected voice, generally, in the field of housing. Its impact
and active concern have been evident in Washington and, also,

at state, county, and municipal levels throughout the country. Although it was but one of many organizations involved in behind-the-scenes and out-front maneuvering during the Congressional debates over the creation of HUD, the work of this trade association, founded in 1942, will be examined in detail to pinpoint its influence and the role of housing lobbies, in general, in the struggle for, and subsequent development of the Department.

Legislative circumstances at the time of its founding during World War II put the NAHB immediately and directly into a lobbying role. Today, this 44,000-member association is recognized as one of the most successful interest groups operating in the nation's capital. The NAHB was formed when the private home-building industry was threatened by tightening war controls, and thus, it was logical that its early work centered on a series of moves to maintain supplies of copper, lumber, and other scarce building materials in the private market to keep the building industry extant, if repressed, despite the war effort. Most of the private housing effort was, naturally, in the field of military housing during the World War II years.

After the war, NAHB trained its guns against public housing. Its positive support was put behind easier government mortgage terms and higher limits on GI loan interest ceilings (originally 3.5 per cent).

By 1951, the Association found itself back almost in the same position in which it had started—fighting war controls, this time during the Korean conflict. At this point, in the early 1950's, its efforts focused, in large measure, on lobbying for more favorable treatment from Congress and the housing agencies, and on getting new members.

Since 1951, NAHB's activities have multiplied and spread into many fields. Today, these include technical and economic research, a consumer information program, long-range planning, sales and training courses, a scholarship program, a wide variety of seminars and conferences on mortgage financing, urban renewal, design, community facilities, and many other of the special aspects of housing. Yet, according to *House and Home* magazine, for January, 1962, "it is hard to dispute that lobbying is still NAHB's No. 1 *raison d'être* and the organization is known as one of the most active and influential lobby groups in Washington."

By association standards, NAHB is still young. *House and Home* also said of it in 1962: "It has come a long way and passed through a difficult adolescence to become a dynamic organization that in many ways reflects the strength and weakness of the giant industry it serves. NAHB may not yet be mature, but it is well along the road to maturity."

In many ways, the bare statistics of NAHB's growth are quite impressive. In 1942, the Association started with 298 members in 13 local chapters. In 1952, there were 25,000 members in 190 chapters. Today, there are about 400 chapters. Of its 44,000 members, about 16,000 are builders, and the other 28,000 include architects, subcontractors, bankers, lumber dealers, suppliers, and other industry people.

NAHB is organized for operation on several levels. The most important, of course, is national. At its Washington headquarters, the 140-man staff carries out policies shaped by the Association's 25-man executive committee and approved by a 700-member board. The president, first vice president, secretary, treasurer, 12 regional vice presidents, the immediate past president, 8 members appointed by the president, and (in a more unofficial way) 2 honorary life members are members of the executive committee.

The executive committee functions as an advisory board to the president and his officers, but in theory, cannot make policy. This capacity, again in theory, is reserved exclusively to the 700-man board of directors, which meets three times each year. This group is chosen to represent the local associations on a proportional basis, and the selection is based on the size of the local group. Fifty national representatives serve as the interim group of advisers for the board, but all final decisions revert to the board.

Obviously, in an organization such as NAHB, much of the

true policy direction and decision-making rests with its president, who traditionally rises through the ranks. As a member of its public information staff has politely phrased it: "Much rests with the personality of the NAHB president."

Liaison with the FHA and VA is, of course, extensive. Builders constantly call from across the country asking for aid in interpreting orders or seeking other assistance that they can get only by contacting the proper government outlet. The NAHB brochure *Join and Profit* says: "Through this liaison you have *direct* representation in Washington at the FHA and VA offices."

NAHB's department of governmental affairs includes the subdivisions of labor and international housing, and, of course, all lobbying activities. NAHB insiders, when pressed, characterize the Association as "a pretty effective lobbying operation," but point out that the group has only three registered lobbyists. One has been executive vice-president since late 1965. The others are two NAHB governmental affairs specialists.

They are backed by a contributing staff of eighty to ninety economists, statisticians, and bankers who report on a monthly basis, giving the Association's economics department a "great fountain of information for the Hill . . . which is much better than the government on projections," according to Association spokesmen.

Keynoting the Association's stance, its public relations director has said, "Over the last 15 to 20 years Congress has recognized that we're lobbying for a special group—housing, but that it's done honestly . . . they have respect for the work being done here . . . negativism is not part of what we're trying to do."

Among the organizations that lined up with NAHB favoring enactment of the enabling legislation for HUD, were the U.S. Conference of Mayors, the National League of Cities, the National Housing Conference, the American Institute of Planners, the American Institute of Architects, the AFL-CIO, the

National Association of Housing and Redevelopment Officials, and the National Association of Mutual Savings Banks.

Opposing enactment were the National Association of Real Estate Boards, the Chamber of Commerce of the United States, and the National Association of Manufacturers. The Mortgage Bankers Association of America imposed severe conditions on approval and was regarded, generally, as contrary.

In 1962, President Kennedy told home builders:

> Your industry is of vital importance to the national economy and vitally important to an increase in the national standard of living; and the relations between government and the housing industry, the partnership which has existed, permitted prosperity for the housing industry, and the well being of our people.

That same year, speaking before the NAHB's board of directors, Kennedy's Secretary of Commerce, Luther Hodges, summarized: "Homebuilding is one of the footings upon which our nation's social and economic welfare is constructed."

The Association's original stance on the question of Cabinet-level representation for the industry had come in then President Martin L. Bartling's address to the Group V Association of Savings Banks in New York in February, 1960:

> Our great political parties should formulate bold and imaginative housing philosophies and spell these out in unequivocal terms. We believe these philosophies should then be given form and substance at the Cabinet level of government—a level where the . . . voice of housing in all of its ramifications may be heard on equal terms with those of Agriculture, of Labor and of the Treasury.

Five months later, on July 11, 1960, Bartling took action and sent the Association's statement of its views of the industry on housing policies to the platform committees of both the Democratic and Republican parties.

The following June, NAHB had a new president. In testimony before committees of the House and Senate, the recently elected E. J. Burke asserted that NAHB could support the bill

(H.R.6433) to create the new department only if it were amended in four important respects. They were: (1) the transfer of FHA as an "intact unit" to the new department instead of abolishing the agency and transferring its functions, powers and duties to the Secretary of the department, (2) inclusion of language in the bill to make it a stated purpose to encourage a prosperous and efficient construction industry, (3) that provisions be made for an under secretary of housing, (4) that the name be "Department of Housing and Urban Affairs." (A reverse wording appeared in the bill.)

In September, 1961, the Senate reacted. Provisions were added to the bill to give increased emphasis on housing—an action, according to the Senate Committee, "intended to allay fears expressed by some witnesses before the committee that the department's principal objective would be community development and redevelopment and that housing and housing construction would be secondary." In essence, this addition served to reassure the home-building industry that private initiative, especially in land acquisition and development, would not take a back seat to government-planned programs.

In January, 1962, another new NAHB president, Leonard L. Frank, dispatched a letter to Representative Howard W. Smith, Democrat of Virginia, and Chairman of the House Rules Committee, expressing NAHB's opposition to H.R.8429, the bill that would create the new department. "During the last session," Frank wrote, "the home building industry supported a general proposal but with serious reservations." He remarked further that "neither the bill as proposed by the Administration nor evidence of future intention as expressed by Administration spokesmen gave adequate recognition to the importance of the present and future housing needs of the country." He went on to note that "the overwhelming production of housing which is needed before the end of this decade and the importance of this task in a new department seemed almost wholly left out of the considerations giving rise to the bill."

In Senate and House testimony a month later, NAHB's Frank reiterated his fears:

Instead of giving it a place at the Cabinet table which the importance of home building and housing needs and wants, statements by Administration spokesmen and advocates of the new department clearly emphasize that the main reason for its creation is to give big cities and their problems an adequate voice in the highest councils of government. . . .

This ended the Association's action on the bill in 1962.

In June, 1963, Frank's successor offered an alternative. In a letter to Senator Edmund Muskie, Maine Democrat, of the Subcommittee on Intergovernmental Relations, he commented that it might be "appropriate to consider the creation of a Presidential office on urban or community affairs to coordinate federal and regional planning activities." He added that "such coordination does not occur fully in the existing federal framework, and it would be difficult for a proposed Department of Urban Affairs, which would be of the same rank as existing departments, to coordinate effectively other agencies' programs."

This suggestion was formalized by Pennsylvania's Republican Senator Hugh Scott. Scott introduced S.1963 (H.R.7835) on August 5, 1963, and said his plan would be more efficient than the defeated Cabinet-level Department of Urban Affairs. "There is much greater need for an executive staff with authority to cut across established bureaucratic lines than for a new bureaucratic establishment," Scott reasoned.

Four months later NAHB urged, in what was, essentially, a new tone:

NAHB is a professional body of professional people, and it must take the lead for community projects and social development. Builders must and will achieve the professional status of doctors and lawyers. This is an NAHB responsibility. The biggest challenge facing NAHB builders is providing housing for the vast middle income market.

The Association's stand remained the same, however:

We continue to oppose establishment of any Cabinet department which would absorb the present housing agencies and functions unless housing is given status therein consistent with its primary importance.

In December, 1964, President Johnson made a notable gesture and telegraphed the NAHB convention in Chicago that the Administration welcomed NAHB's counsel "on how best to solve our housing and community problems." He commended NAHB's "wise leadership," and the industry's "fine partnership" with the federal government.

Within a month, the Administration proposal took form and was publicly announced. The reaction of the GOP was swift. Seizing, in part, on NAHB's 1963 suggestion, Representative William Widnall, New Jersey Republican and a ranking member of the Subcommittee on Housing of the House Banking and Currency Committee, proposed (1) combining Urban Renewal Administration and the Public Housing Administration to eliminate needless duplication in slum clearance, planning, land appraisal, relocation services, personnel, and other activities, (2) creation of an independent FHA, and (3) establishment in the White House of a coordinating and information office to handle urban affairs.

Finally, NAHB, on March 5, 1965, announced:

We favor creation of a Department of Housing and Community Development. Primary recognition should be given to private housing production. This can easily be done in its statement of purposes and structure. A ranking official just below secretarial level should be designated for housing and residential finance. Public loan and grant programs should be separated from private housing functions. FHA and FNMA should remain intact with their heads carrying assistant secretary rank.

This declaration was followed, almost immediately, by the announcement that twenty-four House Republicans were on the record for Widnall's Office of Community Development.

NAHB officers, committee chairmen, and members met for three days in the National Housing Center. They dissected and analyzed proposed legislation and attempted to hammer out guidelines to assist President Perry Willits in testifying, on March 31, before the House committee and, on the Senate side, on April 2.

His statement read in part:

> NAHB has for several years supported the establishment of a Department of Housing and Urban Development provided that housing is given primary recognition in such an executive department. We believe that safeguards must be established within such a department to continue a high level of operation of the Federal Housing Administration and the Federal National Mortgage Association. While the legislation proposed by President Johnson does not spell out precisely what would be the future role of FHA, we would assume that it is the Administration's intent to give it high status and to place major emphasis upon private enterprise in housing and urban development. The official title of the proposed new department would suggest that . . . As for FNMA, we are gratified to note that it would be transferred intact to the new department, indicating that its important and stabilizing functions in the private home financing sector would be continued as at present.

Willits himself spoke before the House and Senate subcommittees on Housing and the subcommittee on Executive Reorganization of the Senate Government Operations Committee on March 31 and April 1 and 2. During the latter hearings, Chairman Ribicoff commented that Willits' suggestion for an amendment to the proposed legislation, which would state that one of the four assistant secretaries to be created within the department would be specifically charged with administration of programs dealing with the private mortgage market, "makes sense."

Later, in what was apparently a victory for the Association, among others, the bill passed the House Government Operations Committee twenty to eight with Willits' suggestion incorporated in the approved amendment introduced by Representative Chet Holifield, California Democrat.

The fight was still on, however, and Association spirits were buoyed when Johnson told an NAHB meeting in May: "We solicit your interest and your support."

On June 9, another obstacle was overcome when the bill was cleared for action as amended by the House Rules Committee, and, later that month, the measure passed the entire House 217 to 184. Commenting on the bill's House passage, Willits remarked:

> It contains also a provision suggested by the NAHB which will insure continuity of the programs now conducted by the FHA and the FNMA. This provision designates one of the four assistant secretaries to be established within the department to administer programs relating to the private mortgage market. In our testimony before the Senate Government Operations Committee we urged that it approve a similar provision. We are confident that the Senate will recognize the validity of the provisions approved by the House.

Senate approval came by a 57-to-33 vote. The bill then went to the conference committee, and the final version contained the following amendment:

> There shall be in the department a Federal Housing Commissioner, who shall be one of the Assistant Secretaries, who shall head a Federal Housing Administration within the Department, who shall have such duties and powers as may be prescribed by the Secretary, and who shall administer, under the supervision and direction of the Secretary, departmental programs relating to the private mortgage market.

In the Rose Garden signing ceremonies in September, 1965, President Johnson remarked that "this is a wise, just and progressive measure for all America, and I am honored to sign it."

Willits, in a statement released for the Association on this occasion, commented,

> We of the home building industry are highly gratified that the problems of housing and urban development are now to be given recognition at the highest level of government.

The NAHB vigorously supported the legislation in its course

through the Congress and we are pleased that it is now law.

The private home building industry has endeavored over the past twenty years to achieve the goal of affording every American family the opportunity for a home of its own on terms that it can afford.

We have worked closely with the federal government toward achieving this goal and we believe such cooperative effort will be further aided by this new recognition of the nation's housing needs and urban development problems.

After the HUD legislation was passed, NAHB continued to have strong relations with the White House during the administration of Larry Blackmon, a Texan and long-time friend of President Johnson and some of his advisers.

During the "tight money" crisis of 1966, Blackmon could always get through to the White House. However, there was no immediate evidence that the fears of the private home builders were leading to executive action. When the effects of tight money slowed housing to a halt, there was action on emergency funds and more FHLBB money for Savings and Loans.

Since Leon N. Weiner was selected NAHB president in late 1966, the Association's big push has been for establishment of a secondary mortgage facility within FNMA for conventional loans and establishment of a HUD assistant secretary just for mortgage finance.

Much of NAHB's current liaison is with Senator John Sparkman's housing subcommittee and, also, with the Federal Reserve Board, the Council of Economic Advisors, and FHLBB. Meetings are held with HUD, but the relationships are not as close as might have been expected.

## HUD's Public Relations

Exercises in better understanding of HUD legislation, programs, and the special where-when-how of project information naturally are the charge of HUD's section on public affairs— the general federal term for public relations, public information, or just plain publicity.

Under the direction of Wayne Phillips, a former New York City reporter, and a Kennedy appointee to an HHFA post with Robert Weaver, this HUD activity has followed the new organizational pattern by coordinating public affairs efforts of FHA and FNMA, for instance, and putting all members of the public relations team on notice that they are working for the full Department, as well as for a particular assistant secretary or program. Besides stepping up the amount of press information and facilities to serve television and radio outlets throughout the United States, this office has had a strong hand in the preparation of many pamphlets and reports to explain new or changed HUD programs.

One particular innovation was the setting up of a first floor information service office in HUD's main office. Many of the information aids are directed to the general public, but a notable service is to the small builder or developer who might have in mind a small college housing project in St. Louis, or something of that sort. Every effort is made to give him the information he needs to get going.

# IX

## How HUD Is Doing:
## Some Pros and Cons

America's continuing and apparently irrevocable trend into urbanization must be considered as the background against which every argument is spotlighted in assessing HUD's achievements or shortcomings. Today, U.S. citizens are living in over 200 metropolitan areas, with more than half of that metropolitan population in the extended urban strips, East and West and elsewhere, that have become known as "megalopolises." For instance, the area stretching from Boston to Washington, D.C., has 40 million residents—and that strip may, indeed, be considered to reach as far north as Kennebunkeport, Maine, and as far south as Key West, Florida.

It is against the disorganized metropolitan community structures that HUD's programs and policies must be judged, and its problems understood.

"HUD has problems," wrote Andrew R. Mandala under a Washington dateline in a trade newspaper called the *Weekly Bond Buyer* on November 21, 1966. "After a full year in existence, the Housing Department—the 11th Cabinet post—still is trying to get out from under one of the greatest bureaucratic bogs Washington has ever seen."

Mandala denied that HUD was about to fall apart and he stressed that strides had been made in the first year. But he insisted that staff morale was low and industry opinion had reached a "rock bottom" level. To the regional offices of

HUD, Mandala attributed quotes such as "We can't get any decisions made when we need them." At the Washington headquarters, it was reported, top staff aids lacked pride in their Department.

Mandala concluded his critical HUD appraisal: "It is thought that if Dr. Weaver permits himself the time, HUD's organizational ball will begin to roll in earnest. But even with a concerted effort toward filling the gaps that exist, it will probably be another year before the Department shakes itself into an effective force for urban development."

However, the same day that HUD was chastised by the *Weekly Bond Buyer,* it could point to a story headlined "HUD Shows Promise on Birthday" in *The Washington Post.* This article by White House reporter William Chapman noted that HUD had got its model cities program—"a genuinely novel approach to urban rebuilding"—through Congress and had "melded five autonomous and frequently warring agencies into a semblance of unity." Chapman reported that the nation's big city mayors were generally delighted with the new HUD. Mayor Ralph Locher of Cleveland was quoted as saying that public housing officials were "much more cooperative" after being moved under the HUD roof. And Mayor Henry Maier of Milwaukee said that he found urban renewal applications moving faster.

FHA MORTGAGE USE

One of the most useful tools HUD has at its disposal is the FHA mortgage. In many urban programs, it is the principal credit aid.

There is some disagreement in the private sector about the transfer, or extension, of the long-appreciated FHA mortgage insurance from the field of single housing to the rebuilding of cities. Certain spokesmen would have FHA restrict its basic financing role to insuring economically sound residences—as it has been doing successfully and without cost to the taxpayers for more than thirty years.

Another view takes the stand that the original role of FHA has become obsolete because government help no longer is needed in the private field, where sound and liberal financing arrangements are now available within the conventional mortgage money market. With FHA now part of the mortgage credit section of the HUD complex, this view holds that the FHA mortgage financing role should not rest on its record of success and cling to its proven markets and risks. Rather, since FHA has already influenced the conventional mortgage field to an extent that there is only a slight gap between them, the right approach for HUD mortgage credit is to open up new markets and opportunities with private resources.

One particular program continues to move ahead despite the swirl of controversy it has attracted since its inception in 1961. The 221(d)(3) program of below-market-interest-rate mortgages, originally designed to promote the construction of housing for low- and mid-income families who earned too much to qualify for public housing but still found themselves outpriced when seeking to buy shelter in the private market, has been broadened to include the handicapped, the elderly, and persons displaced by government renewal projects.

When programs are financed, generally at about 3 per cent interest, special assistance funds are used and the FHA insurance premium is waived. This so-called submarket technique has been criticized as a violation of the cost-benefit balance. Its opponents charge that this program represents a subsidy from the Fannie Mae secondary mortgage market operations. The complaint from the private mortgage banking field has been that this is an example of programs that have become substitutes, rather than supplements, for private mortgage money.

Businessmen admit, however, that FHA-insured financing has already made possible completed urban renewal projects of widely varying types. One company, the Reynolds Metals Development Corporation cites two projects—River Park in the nation's capital and Parade Park in Kansas City, Missouri

—as examples of what can be achieved through business-government cooperation, with FHA mortgage banking.

River Park, in Washington's Southwest urban renewal area, is a showplace development of 134 townhouses of striking barrel-vault-roof design and 384 high-rise apartments. A cooperative project designed for middle-income residents, River Park townhouses sold in a range from $1,300 to $1,600 in down payments with monthly charges ranging from $167 to $219. Apartment down payments varied from $700 for an efficiency to $1,100 for a two-bedroom unit, with monthly charges from $85 to $175.

On the other side of the cost spectrum, the 550-home Parade Park in Kansas City was designed specifically for moderate-income families. It was financed under FHA's 221(d)(3) provisions and resulted in some of the lowest costs found in urban renewal areas. The Parade Park cooperative has sold two- and three-bedroom townhouses for initial investments of $125 and $150 respectively, and monthly charges of $69.50 and $79.50. In addition, Reynolds built without additional charge a $75,000 community building from savings in construction costs. Other Reynolds, FHA-financed renewal projects are in Philadelphia, Cincinnati, Baltimore. Syracuse, Providence, Hartford, and Richmond.

## STRESS ON REHABILITATION

Secretary Weaver once pointed out to a questioner that the urban renewal approach is being changed under new HUD programs, citing the clearance of 500 former slum acres in the Southwest sector of Washington, D.C., as an example of earlier (1949–55) style renewal that predicated reconstruction on total clearance. The new housing attracted higher-income groups rather than those who had previously been living in the area.

Weaver said that the new approach is to give a balance to the program by placing more stress on rehabilitation. He cited the Shaw School area in a predominantly Negro sector of

Washington's inner city as one in which the same income groups and same people will be rehoused through a program of rehabilitation of existing residential structures. "There'll be spot clearance and some new construction," he said, "but there will be a minimum of displacement and a minimum of relocation."

When HUD had been in existence for about a year, a spokesman for the National Association of Home Builders was asked to assess housing's place at the Cabinet table. NAHB president Larry Blackmon said, merely: "We are still waiting for our voice to be heard."

Home builders—who put their weight behind the federal impetus for HUD's Cabinet seat—are not altogether satisfied that the new Department is giving as much attention to "housing" as to "urban development."

### Decline in Housing Starts

Yet a fair assessment of the sharp decline in residential construction during 1966 (from about 1.5 million total units to about 1.1 million) does not reflect discredit on anybody or anything within the power of HUD itself. The mortgage money market became stringent early in 1966, and housing starts fell off. The mortgage money pinch could not be laid at the threshhold of HUD, but NAHB officials did often express their dissatisfaction with the lack of special help provided by the Johnson Administration. And, occasionally, NAHB indicated that it felt HUD might have made a stronger stand to obtain more federal funds for the housing market.

(Larry Blackmon, the Fort Worth builder whose term as NAHB president ended late in 1966, often took his pleas for more government financial aid directly to his fellow Texan and personal friend in the White House. And on the opening day of the NAHB convention in December, 1966, Blackmon indicated that President Johnson would order the release of funds from the Federal Home Loan Bank Board to the conventional mortgage market for new home loans. Three days after the convention opened in Chicago, President Johnson announced the release of $500 million from the FHLBB for home loans. Blackmon said: "That's the amount he said it would be.")

Blackmon and Weaver have agreed that America really needs 2 million new homes each year to take care of housing needs. On the subject of the desirable rate of home construction, Weaver has said:

> The demographers told me in 1961 that we were going to have this new family formation (surge) in 1962. And then in 1962 they told me we were going to have it in 1963. And in 1963 they told me we were going to have it in 1964. So I've been a little shy about the numbers game since that time. I would say that I think in the not too distant future we're going to have something like 2 million starts a year to meet our requirements and this is almost double what we're doing today.

### The Secretary Criticized

When the private housing industry declined to alarming levels in late 1966, few strong criticisms were hurled directly at Secretary Weaver. However, private comment and some that found its way into housing trade journals made it clear there was a strong feeling that the HUD Secretary had been too silent publicly as the debate grew over housing's priority in the economy. In particular, the NAHB was disappointed that more support had not been given to its varied recommendations for federal help by the man at the President's Cabinet table. Yet, it was granted that Secretary Weaver had to maintain his loyalty as a member of the Johnson Administration.

Secretary Weaver has, of course, fully supported Presidential orders and directives on human rights and equal opportunities. Yet, the dislocation of low-income families by urban renewal has brought undeserved criticism to his door—the same door on which some racially biased home builders have dumped their criticisms that HUD has been moving too far in its wide-ranging new programs involving neighborhoods and social conditions.

Any federal housing program—one with federal aid—is charged with providing nondiscriminatory housing opportunity for all people.

## Creative Partnership

An official of the National Association of Real Estate Boards has pointed out that the history of the federal government's relationship to its cities can be divided into three eras: (1) from the founding until 1932, when there had been only incidental dealings with cities; (2) the era of the Reconstruction Finance Corporation and succeeding New Deal programs, which authorized federal help to cities and people via economic recovery and urban programs; and (3) the period beginning with the creation of the Department of Housing and Urban Development in 1965. He reasoned that:

> For good or for ill, this third period merged the scattered tubes of Federal connection to the cities into a major pipe line. The future will show that housing as a sphere of influence, however extensive it may be, will not have the dominant position in the activities of the new Department of Housing and Urban Development that the word "housing" may imply in the initial name of the new cabinet agency. The new department is for a more telling Federal impact on the cities.

Spokesmen for the private sector of the housing and finance industries have spelled out their recognition that urban revitalization requires the federal government to maintain its role in a balanced perspective to the contribution of free enterprise. A representative of the National Association of Mutual Savings Banks, has said that he believes it is essential

> for private enterprise to recognize that the Federal Government does have a key function to perform in the building and rebuilding of our urban environment. What we must establish, in essence, is a creative partnership between the private

and public sectors, parallel to the 'creative Federalism' envisioned with respect to Federal and state and local governments. Such a partnership will seek the realization of broadly accepted public goals through maximum use of private means.

## PROBLEMS AND PROGRAMS

There can be no doubt that HUD officials are well aware of such problems as vandalism in public housing projects and recognize that lack of regard for a landlord's property (either in government or private ownership) can best be overcome by making the destructive forces become constructive through the hope of a new way of life. But to bring the impoverished and the spiritless into active roles, there must be effective training for personal participation in rehabilitation efforts. One difficulty is the reluctance of the building trade unions and private contractors to become actively involved either in such training programs or in the rehabilitation work itself. To join in the rebuilding, the unions and the contractors would have to overturn old municipal building codes that often rule out the use of new and lower cost rehabilitation tools, such as prefabricated plumbing units with plastic piping.

Despite all the problems, HUD's quest for cost-saving techniques to assist private industry in the construction of low-income, multilevel housing continues. A new grant of $239,000 went to the Illinois Institute of Technology and Research to adapt advanced European techniques to American construction methods in an effort to create more efficient patterns of high-rise construction. The main experiment will use single-unit combinations of whole walls, walls and ceilings, walls and floors, and ceilings and floors to evaluate cost reductions. The Secretary announced: "This Chicago demonstration will help us to develop cost cutting and time saving construction methods that can be widely used throughout the country."

HUD has recognized that unscrupulous contractors have moved into urban areas and taken unfair advantage of some owners who have been convinced by local planning authorities that their properties need rehabilitating. Both excessively high prices and shoddy workmanship have been observed and the local authority is usually helpless to control the details of a private contract between owner and entrepreneur, who may prove to be unscrupulous.

Therefore, certain features of Section 115 and 312 programs have been designed to protect both owner and local interests by providing local administration under the sponsorship of HUD agencies. Also, inspections have been specified and the local authority is now present when the work contract is signed. Competitive bids are sought, and contractors are screened. Both the local authority and the FHA make inspections during construction. Most important is the handling of loan arrangements and disbursements by the local authority, which does not pay for the work until an inspection warrants it.

One of the major opportunities for these new loans to be workable exists within the framework of cities that have approved urban renewal projects or code enforcement programs. Those cities may make loans and grants to eligible property owners without further action in the sponsoring HUD framework. Information on such projects is available to cities by writing or applying directly to the urban renewal division of HUD headquarters in Washington or to any of the regional offices. HUD officials regard the new rehabilitation loan and grant programs as having a favorable potential to assist cities in fighting blight and preserving older neighborhoods on the brink of blight but essentially worth saving.

However, the neighborhood rehabilitation loan program, with its $100 million authorization for low-interest loans, has been criticized. In Cleveland, the *Plain Dealer* newspaper said the rules are "strangling the operation in its cradle" and claimed that the loans are for people in financial need, but the credit risk stipulations are too high. Another criticism involved three-page application blanks "which only a Philadelphia lawyer could fill out." Further, the *Plain Dealer* editorial (March,

1966) charged that only one application was approved despite the efforts of a staff of eight persons trying to help some home owners.

In fact, the first Cleveland loan went to a couple in the University-Euclid area, who used the $1,130 for exterior and interior work on the house in which they had lived for ten years, and it was reported later that 450 homeowners in that urban renewal area had been declared eligible for Section 115 grants.

In a HUD report to the President, Secretary Weaver noted that private sponsors of housing had developed plans, early in 1967, for a "reserved" status on $13.7 million in construction on 285 projects in 202 different cities. Those projects would house 33,000 families, of which 19,353 would be on the rent supplement basis. Altogether, proposals for rent supplement units totaled 45,000 early in 1967.

## Rent Supplement Use

The first rent supplement contract was signed for a 21-unit project in Cleveland, where rehabilitation was done on two substandard buildings. The income limit in Cleveland for a family of four, under rent supplement, is $4,400 a year. Tenants pay $40 to $60 a month in rent. (The average U.S. supplement payment is less than $50 a month per family.) Prior to the Cleveland rehabilitation, the families had been paying about $85 a month for substandard housing.

Within six months after the rent supplement program was funded by the Congress, nearly sixty projects were receiving payments. Two of the projects operating with some of the $2 million voted for rent supplement were in the Ohio cities of Lorain and Oberlin, both of which came under Section 231, providing housing for the elderly. FHA officials conceded that the program was somewhat slow getting under way due to normal red tape associated with the inauguration of a pioneering effort.

Both profit and nonprofit organizations have been attracted

to the fields of low-income housing, and some of the projects have combined housing for the elderly or moderate-income housing under 221(d)(3) with rent supplement by using a certain number of apartments in a project for middle-income families and other units for low-income families on the rent supplement plan. FHA officials are confident that private developers will respond to this program, which offers a stipulated profit (about 10 per cent as the normal entrepreneur's incentive).

Sponsors interested in developing a rent supplement project can arrange a preliminary conference with the FHA insuring director in their area before making definite plans or commitments for land or professional services. However, the sponsors, limited to nonprofit or corporative entities, must be able to identify the locality and general site area and also be able to identify the type and number of living units to be included and the group or groups the housing is intended to serve. If that information is provided before the preliminary conference, the FHA insuring office is better able to offer suggestions. From the preliminary meeting on, the sponsor can follow procedures outlined in a new handbook that answers questions about rent supplement projects and also outlines further procedures to be followed in obtaining approval.

### Grants for Many Purposes

In justifying its new programs, HUD frequently cites those that combine community planning with fresh ideas. One such planning project involves a $45,000 grant to Peoria, Illinois, to advance the development of techniques to use air rights over ground-level transportation systems and also to provide access to a river front area now isolated by man-made barriers. Another aspect of the program would develop means of handling pleasure boats at docks and screening some of the river front railroad facilities from nonindustrial activities.

Programs initiated and supported by HUD are also designed to allay urban sprawl and to contribute open space for recreation, conservation, and historic appreciation. In Anchorage, Alaska, the objective is to create a "greenbelt" that may shape the future growth of that Northern city. In Detroit, a HUD grant has been made to help purchase and develop a six-acre tract for use as a recreation area in a high-density neighborhood.

Altogether, grants were made within one calendar year to 277 localities to purchase more than 40,000 acres of open land in 35 states. Yet, one of those grants—to suburban Maryland areas near Washington, D.C.—created some resentment of the HUD power itself. While Montgomery County, Maryland, was undergoing a nightmare of rezonings by a lame-duck county council, HUD suspended grant approvals involving millions of dollars until the county reinstated a sound comprehensive area plan that some of those rezoning actions had violated—thus breaking a requirement condition for those grants. County officials, plus Senator Daniel Brewster, Maryland Democrat, charged that HUD was applying muscle in a local controversy. HUD reviewed its position, reinstating some approvals found not to have been adversely affected but standing by others regarded as violating the over-all metropolitan plan for the county.

Another HUD program, part of the FHA administrative operation of Assistant Secretary P. N. Brownstein, was initiated in 1965 to induce planners of subdivisions to put utility wires underground, "where feasible." The burden of proof is on the builder or developer to show that a given installation is not feasible. However, pre-sale agreements in conflict with the underground wiring ruling are given consideration as are extensions of overhead service to new homes in existing subdivisions where that is the established pattern. Brownstein emphasized that new satellite subdivisions in the planning stage must put their wires underground to qualify for FHA mortgage insurance. "It all boils down to this," he said to a group of home builders, "we must check the spread of overhead wires or live like spiders at the center of our webs."

Concern with the aesthetics of residential living also extends to spiritual values of the American tradition. Guidelines for successful local historic preservation have been published by HUD. More than a hundred communities have used HUD programs to halt destruction of historic places. Preservation has been a major theme of urban renewal in Plymouth, Massachusetts, near Plymouth Rock. The Summer and High streets project includes most of historic Burial Hill, the original town square, and Town Brook Valley where most of the early colonial settlements stood. The town had acquired some properties in a piecemeal fashion before federal urban renewal assistance was sought. With federal aid and a renewal plan based on historic preservation, the town tore down some inferior buildings and not only saved but enhanced some of the prime buildings, such as the Richard Sparrow House, built about 1640.

*For Better Design*

The need for better design has been recognized and encouraged by the FHA in recent years. An associate director for design was established in the Architectural Standards Division, and an honors program for residential design, initiated by FHA, now administered by HUD, was inaugurated in 1963. These signs indicate that HUD can be expected to do more in the fields of housing design and site planning through the FHA Renewal and Housing Assistance programs.

The "mediocre quality" of U.S. housing design and sites has been attacked by many. In *Design of the Housing Site, a Critique of American Practice,* a University of Illinois team reported in 223 illustrated pages that its study of 700 housing sites in 30 cities found widespread use of cheap building materials and slapdash construction, in addition to unimaginative siting and utilization of open spaces. Criticisms also included lack of residential privacy and poor provisions for parking and storage of the family car. Mixed residential and commercial uses of land was recommended.

Home builders and developers, as well as federal agencies concerned with housing, have become accustomed to scholarly criticism. Since this University of Illinois report had the benefit of FHA and Urban Renewal Administration financing (before HUD) plus that of the Mobile Homes Manufacturing Association, it was doubly interesting that the report's flyleaf also carried the disclaimer that the findings do "not necessarily represent or coincide with the standards or policy of the Federal Housing Administration," and that Secretary Weaver said: "This book provides a much-needed new perspective in design of the dwelling environment. It shows the numerous ways through which sensitive design can add substantially to the quality of housing in areas of multifamily housing."

# X

# Where HUD Is Heading

How well do you live?

Unfortunately, for too many people in today's urban United States, the answer to this question cannot be one that satisfies the national conscience.

Although strenuous efforts are being made to overcome the problems—of overcrowding, of decayed buildings, of ugliness, of too much noise, of too little transit at reasonable prices, of poor sanitation, of air and water pollution, of social stress and racial tension—the magnitude and complexity of the obstacles to decent urban living for all are of a staggering magnitude and complexity.

Whether the rebuilding of urban facilities and the rehabilitation and extending of living space is to be concentrated inside existing cities or on previously undeveloped land, HUD has the task of setting the standards and leading the way. The words the younger Christopher Wren selected for his architect father's tombstone in St. Paul's cathedral in the heart of London express the spirit Secretary Weaver is plainly trying to instill in his agency associates, and in the urban planners and builders and concerned citizens of the country: "If you would see his monument, look around."

There is hope within HUD itself, and among dedicated professionals in the urban renewal and housing fields outside government, that the latter part of this century will produce worthy monuments in new planned cities and towns, in the design of new or the rehabilitation of aging residential areas

153

and public facilities. The challenge is to build as much or more than has been constructed in three centuries of life in the United States.

"We hope that in years to come men will be able to look around and find in the cities and urban areas across this nation the conditions appropriate to a Great Society," said Secretary Weaver at the cornerstone laying for the new HUD headquarters building in Washington. "We recognize that when that goal is compared to the conditions of today the task ahead is the most ambitious any nation ever set for itself."

## IN HOUSING

Only a year after the creation of the Department of Housing and Urban Development, the Secretary stated: "The goal to which we would attain was outlined in the Housing Act of 1949, which called for a 'decent home and a suitable living environment for every American family.' . . . We seek to create . . . a housing supply . . . of sufficient magnitude and diversity to satisfy the requirements of our people in all economic ranges."

Those words, spoken in November, 1966, to the convening Mortgage Bankers Association, capture the essence of the federal commitment in housing. But, however broad-ranging and adequately funded the HUD programs may be, the creation of a balanced housing supply in this century will require a highly sophisticated mix of economic-social mortars.

Secretary Weaver has estimated that the United States must erect more than 21 million new housing units within the next decade to accomplish the long-sought housing goal regarded as fundamental to a prosperous and healthy citizenry. Approximately 13 million of those new residential dwellings are expected to be basic structures accommodating from one to four families, with the majority single-family houses. Nearly 8 million other units would be in multifamily housing, large garden apartment buildings, medium-size elevator buildings, and towering apartments with banks of high speed elevators.

Services to occupants of rental buildings will range from basic utilities and disposal services for sanitary control to those of the luxury complexes that offer swimming pools, shopping, secretarial service, and plush recreation rooms as part of a newly popular city-within-a-city concept.

The complexity of the nation's housing dream goal emerges clearly when one considers that somewhere between 3 and 6 million of the new housing units, places where people can live in dignity and comfort, must be built for Americans with moderate or low incomes. At present, many of these families are unable to grapple with the financial challenge of home ownership. Already staggering under the inexorable monthly payment demands of installment purchases of clothing and home appliances, and without even a modest rainy-day savings account, they can only try to pay the monthly rent on time and anticipate the day when they may be able to pay more rent for a better residential unit. For these Americans, HUD's 221(d)(3) and rent supplement programs offer the greatest measure of hope in the next decade for a better place to live. Secretary Weaver counseled the nation's mortgage bankers to recognize that a fair percentage of necessary housing must be designed to satisfy "a requirement which is not immediately responsive to market forces." Basically, this statement can be translated to mean that some people cannot be expected to be able to pay their own way in the competitive housing market. Thus, government—federal, state, and local —faces the alternative of supplying some assistance.

In its deepest sense, such an approach to better housing for all persons is an extension of the first federal effort in the provision of FHA-insured mortgages to bring ownership within the range of millions of families who previously had been excluded from the private housing market. The new program poses an economic challenge involving the task of finding methods of employing both thrift and deposit savings for the creation of much-needed housing that will not be owner-occupied. Conventional investing institutions must continue to play an active role in housing but, at the same time, new ways must be developed to bring in nonmortgage funds, such as pensions and individual savings. It has been suggested that a "rethinking of the entire process, both private and public," be made in order to attract more savings into the financing of dwelling units.

A spokesman for the private mortgage money market has said that the federal government has been content to live with a "housing policy that not only permits but nourishes instability." Oliver H. Jones, director of research of the Mortgage Bankers Association, pointed out that the turn of the cycle from easy to tight mortgage credit usually leaves bankruptcies, unsold houses, and poor quality mortgages in its wake. He said that the nation's "objective of decent housing for every family, or the more extensive objective of rebuilding its cities, needs a strong and growing housing industry," which, in his opinion, "is not going to develop within a housing policy that nourishes instability in the demand for its product. This has been the record of the postwar years, including the most recent periods of monetary ease and restraint."

Whenever such criticisms are made, and the whole federal role in housing is questioned, old federal housing hands are likely to recall that the now highly respected and widely utilized FHA had to weather an early barrage of criticism for its implications of "creeping socialism." When the FHA rent supplement program began to be debated, opponents quickly branded it "instant socialism." Yet, HUD officials note, both the National Association of Home Builders and, finally, the more conservative National Association of Real Estate Boards have come to support the rent supplement program. In reply to NAREB's protests, at the beginning of the rent supplement program, against the use of government funds, HUD officials stressed the provision that the housing to be provided will be privately built, privately owned, and privately financed, and pointed out that federal funds were being used only to get the program started, with long-term, permanent private financing expected to follow.

HUD officialdom insists that all the new programs of urban rebuilding and rehabilitation, once they prove to be economically sound, will attract private investment money—as did the old FHA programs. There can be little doubt that the partnership between private industry and government will continue in the field of housing and urban redevelopment simply because neither segment is capable of doing the job alone. Thus, continuation and expansion of mutual efforts can be expected because there is no satisfactory alternative to the cooperation that should conveniently satisfy both interests. And President Johnson has promised that he will encourage, by means of legislative proposals, even more effective cooperation between government and industry for the benefits of owners, tenants, and the industry.

The dual importance of FHA and FNMA may be illustrated to a greater extent than yet realized in future residential mortgage financing programs dependent on marketability of FHA-insured mortgages. More use is expected to be made of FHA's below-market interest rate program of 221(d)(3) rental housing program for builders catering to low-income families. But there is some evidence, too, that more small builder interest will be shown in FHA's 221(d)(4) program that has been liberalized to aid in providing homes for displaced families and moderate-income families. The project may be small (5) units or large (up to a total mortgage of $12½ million) and may be in or out of an urban renewal area. With increasing population in the big cities and the over-all HUD effort to revamp multifamily housing and neighborhoods, it is expected that builders will retreat somewhat from the highly competitive single-family, subdivision-style housing project into these multifamily areas where market conditions show that quick rentals and low vacancy rates can be expected. And because the President and HUD are dedicated to the creation of more low- and moderate-income housing, builders can expect FHA cooperation in faster processing to avoid the delays, red tape, and bureaucratic snarls so often associated with governmental activities.

The rent supplement program might be considered illustrative of the coordination of federal and private efforts. Assistant HUD Secretary Brownstein recently pointed out to the National Association of Home Builders that President Johnson had said: "With supplements paid by their Government, the private builders will be able to move into the low-income housing field which they have not been able to penetrate or to serve effectively in the past."

Brownstein noted, late in 1966, that preliminary reservations of rent supplement funds were made to projects in 112 cities and that the supplements would amount to about $9 million for more than 13,000 units of housing. He emphasized that the program would include small cities, citing that a 12-unit project has been set up for Bloomer, Wisconsin, a town of about 3,000 far removed from metropolitan centers. Yet, Brownstein contended that the significance of the rent supplement program is not location in particular cities—"for it has been my experience there are enough poor to go around—but rather that there now is a means of using the impact of private enterprise on the problem of providing housing for the poor."

Despite the 1967 setback for the program in Congress, most spokesmen for the private sector of the housing and mortgage banking fields have approved the idea of rent supplements because maximum reliance has been allotted to the private sectors for construction, ownership, financing, and management.

## In Urban Development

In an appraisal of HUD, Charles T. Stewart of NAREB wrote:

> Much of the federal government's impact on cities has been in programs designed to remedy defects in established urban areas. In the future we can expect a more concerted federal effort to influence the manner in which land in outlying areas around metropolitan centers is developed or withdrawn from possible development under the banner of open space.

Already, local governments are being helped by HUD programs to purchase undeveloped tracts to be maintained as
parkland open space to curb urban sprawl, and, concurrently,
provide room for outdoor recreation for urban and suburban
citizens. NAREB's Stewart, a former executive director of the
Urban Land Institute, also pointed out that, although the
satellite city, a self-contained unit with relationship to a large
city, has not been the child of government programs, "there
is clearly federal interest in bringing this new pattern of urbanization under federal influence."

More efforts to coordinate metropolitan areas to avoid the
difficulties that local governments have in providing new
planning on a totality basis can be expected. Already, the
federal inducements of funds for planning, mass transit, open
space, and new sewer facilities have given progressive and
growing areas exceptional opportunities to accomplish the
broad-scale, coordinated planning made necessary by modern
problems.

How much will be spent by the federal government in rebuilding its cities and setting up a climate for the creation of
new towns and satellite cities? An estimate of $1 trillion was
set forth by Senator Abraham Ribicoff early in 1967 when he
again called for a $50 billion ten-year program to get the job
done. He suggested that the private sector of activity could
handle the effort with government cooperation (principally
financial aid) at all levels. The Senator also proposed that
HUD establish an agency to cut the cost of housing construction in half. If that can be done, HUD will merit a nickname
as "the Miracle Department."

As a matter of fact, there are many miracles to be per-
formed by HUD if the vast aims of urban renewal policies are
to be met—in code enforcement, implementation of the broad-
scale rent supplement program, fulfillment of planning for
instant rehabilitation of solid structures that have become
slums, relocation of families and businesses displaced by urban
renewal, development of new concepts for transit within cities,

as well as the creation of new towns in regions where metropolitan areas are sprawling into each other's outer precincts.

It is hoped that the planned communities of Reston, Virginia, on 6,800 acres, and Columbia, Maryland, on 14,000 acres, located within 25 miles of HUD's own new headquarters, will be answers to the "scatteration" problem outlined by Edmund K. Faltermayer in an article in *Fortune* (September, 1966). He charged that the United States "has virtually ceased creating new settlements that have focal points of the traditional type, with stores, offices, schools and churches closely linked by sidewalks," citing what the developer of Columbia City and new president of Urban America, Inc., James W. Rouse, called "non-communities," formless places without order, beauty, or reason, "created," according to Faltermayer, "by an irrational process that shows no visible respect for people or land."

At Columbia, the Rouse group hopes to see a new city for approximately 100,000 people completed by about 1980, with homes, apartments, industries, stores, lakes, schools, libraries, hospitals, hotels, restaurants, and other elements of livability. The site, on rolling farmland midway between Washington and Baltimore along Route 29, already has been granted a $50 million mortgage commitment from commercial sources. It is likely that the private residential development of Columbia will participate in HUD programs to provide housing for middle- and low-income families.

As noted earlier, developer Robert E. Simon already has qualified his Reston new city for a HUD demonstration housing grant for lower-income families. Opened in 1964, Reston built its first village around man-made Lake Anne, with townhouses, apartments, a high-rise residential building, and a commercial section that has apartments above the shops near the lake. On larger lots, flanking out from the first lake, Reston has single-family dwellings and varied clusters of other townhouses. Many of the homes are built around a golf course that was opened before any homes were completed. At the end of 1966, Reston had more than 6,000 residents and several going industries in its garden park development area. And hundreds of builder-developers have visited Reston for information to guide their own new town planning.

Similar new towns and cities are planned or are under construction across the country. Ground has been broken for the large-scale community of Litchfield in Arizona. Two other cities, Hamilton near San Francisco and Valencia in Southern California, are described as "in the planning stage." Smaller towns, with claims to planned, full living status, are under way in many parts of the nation—particularly in the West and Southwest. Although not a new-town idea in the generally accepted mold, the Rossmoor "Leisure World" offers an enclave development for persons over fifty years of age. Several such large communities have been successfully developed near San Francisco and Los Angeles. Others have been opened near Washington, D.C., and between Philadelphia and New York City. No provisions are made for children or schools in these self-styled leisure worlds, but home ownership in low-lying residential structures is offered on a forty-year, FHA-insured basis of cooperative ownership, with Leisure World providing maintenance, golf courses, pools, recreation centers, and hospital facilities for fees that are part of the amortization payments. The Rossmoor concept is designed to attract still active retirees and couples anticipating retirement.

Leisure World's Ross Cortese is one of the nation's largest builder developers, but not as big and experienced as William J. Levitt, whose techniques have been a revolutionary force in the industry, and whose annual home-building pace now exceeds 5,000 in locations ranging from Long Island to Puerto Rico. Over its first thirty-five years, the Levitt firm has concentrated on modestly priced suburban single housing recently without FHA financing. But now there are many signs that Levitt and other major builders will be designing and building large, complete urban settlements within the next decade. Speaking from his own considerable experience with large subdivisions with some community services, shopping, schools, pools, and churches—in the New York City, Philadelphia, and Washington areas, Levitt said: "Land close enough to the cities for people to get to work has mostly been used up. The small area remaining is snarled by restrictions and priced out of sight. The only solution is to create jobs where there is open land and to provide housing close to those jobs."

Thus, it would not surprise housing professionals if the Levitt firm were to acquire large tracts of undeveloped land near, but not adjacent to, major cities and embark on a program of new towns or cities. The likelihood is that any large new town developer will be a participant in present or future HUD programs to provide housing and related community services for low- and moderate-income families, who supply the manpower needed by industry and business. More and more, America's builders and developers will be encouraged by their own philosophy and by HUD programs to provide what developer Rouse has set as his own goal at Columbia: "Housing for everybody from the janitor to the chairman of the board."

## WITH OUTSIDE HELP

An organization expected to act as a catalyst in reshaping the American city with the cooperation of both federal programs and private initiative, is the relatively new Urban America, Inc., whose central mission is "to establish a constructive discontent with the way we are building urban areas today and to introduce a new order into the process of urban growth."

Funded through the philanthropic support of the late Stephen R. Currier, and headed by a blue-ribbon group of officers, Urban America is the result of a merger of the American Planning and Civic Association and the Action Council for Better Cities, and is based in Washington, D.C. Its specific aims, such as the application of better standards of urban design to new developments, the preservation of valuable older urban structures, and the conservation of open space in metropolitan areas, although distinct and with their own nuances, are not likely to clash philosophically with the goals of the HUD team. Its varied activities (including publication of *Architectural Forum,* planning of national conferences, and exerting influence on urban rebuilding) seem to have the same general direction as, and to support, HUD.

One of Urban America's most practical programs, and an example of the help that HUD is getting from related sources outside its jurisdiction, is its local development service. In support of this service to localities and builders, Urban America has recently published *Nonprofit Housing: Illustrative Case,* a 360-page loose-leaf guide for nonprofit housing sponsors to lead them through the more than sixty highly technical forms involved in processing a 221(d)(3) loan from HUD-FHA. The book contains all the required FHA forms, filled out in detail with data found in a typical new construction project. The attorney authors (John R. Gallagher, III, and John J. O'Donnell, Jr.) give the purpose of each form and list special precautions that should be taken in completing it. The Urban America staff is pledged to update the book to reflect changes in FHA procedures or legislative amendments. An introductory section lists conditions under which sponsors may qualify and also discusses the differences between loans at below-market interest rate and those at market rate. Guidelines include information on FHA formulas for rent schedules and mortgage limitations and also tenant selection, management of projects, and the use of project income.

Not only are such nonprofit organizations expected to help HUD move ahead. Private businesses of many sorts have begun, also, to channel men and money and imagination into joint projects with the federal Department, or into backing its policies.

As *The Wall Street Journal* recently noted, in Pittsburgh, Pennsylvania, ACTION-Housing, Inc., a housing rehabilitation group that is an offshoot of a development fund financed by major banks and businesses, has taken a public stand that the rent subsidy program is essential to provide decent housing for the poor. Other businessmen's organizations and private industry are actively supporting other HUD programs.

In 1967, HUD Secretary Weaver presented the Department's Urban Pioneer Medal to Graham J. Morgan, president of U.S. Gypsum Company, for that firm's "daring and keen perception to channel the experience, insights, and efficiencies of private enterprise into the field of residential rehabilitation." Under Morgan's leadership and the supervision of salesman turned project manager Warren Obey, U.S. Gypsum undertook a $1.6 million project in six tenement buildings on 102d Street in New York City. The project was developed in cooperation with a city housing agency and HUD. Private financing was insured by the FHA under its experimental housing program for mortgage insurance on properties using new or untried construction concepts aimed at reducing housing costs, raising living standards, and improving neighborhood design. FHA issued its first commitment for insurance on the U.S. Gypsum project in May, 1966, and rehabilitation began shortly thereafter.

In accepting the medal, the U.S. Gypsum president said that the firm was enlarging its rehabilitation commitment in Harlem and making plans for pilot studies in other large city slum areas. Morgan said that his firm had learned how to use low-cost, incombustible wall partitions in the Harlem rehabilitation which eventually will be insured by a long-term FHA 221(d)(3) loan. Morgan also noted that rents were being kept moderately low under the New York City rent ceilings by virtue of tax abatement incentives for renewal, as well as by the 3 per cent interest rate for a 221(d)(3) loan. The hundreds of inquiries U.S. Gypsum has had from private companies and nonprofit organizations interested in similar projects promise well for future expansion of such activities.

Related efforts in this field have been under way for several years within the National Association of Home Builders, which provides its members with "can do" information on all topics relating to multifamily development construction and financing, much of it eligible under HUD programs for federal assistance. Other private groups in the housing industry also are engaged in translating federal housing program specifications into this-is-how-it-can-be-done information for interested individuals, companies, and cities.

## WITH INTERGOVERNMENTAL COOPERATION

Charged with making his office "the generating source of innovation and experimental development," the assistant secretary for Demonstrations and Intergovernmental Relations also has the obligation to supervise the code studies division of HUD and make studies of housing and building codes, zoning regulations and development standards. One effort in this direction brought the assignment of former Senator Paul H. Douglas to head a national commission that will make a thorough study of American cities and urban areas—reviewing zoning, housing and building codes, taxation, and development standards. The commission is expected to recommend solutions to increase the supply of low-cost, decent housing for Americans.

In another direction, HUD and Assistant Secretary Taylor assigned a $174,000 federal urban renewal demonstration grant to the Commonwealth of Massachusetts to underwrite two-thirds of the cost of new methods of relocating families and businesses displaced by various government actions. In this activity with the Bay State and with HUD's own urban renewal division, Taylor has further opportunity to show how new cooperation can be brought to the broad problems of intergovernmental relations. Taylor also coordinates local housing market studies and develops information on the national housing and mortgage markets related to economic questions as part of his Office of Economic and Market Analysis.

The range of Taylor's Demonstrations and Intergovernmental Relations' responsibility is as broad as any within

HUD. As the Assistant Secretary has said, "We are in a new ball game. In fact, we are in a new ball park. . . . There never has been a federal program of this scope, magnitude, and opportunity for the cities."

Assistant Secretary Taylor has also said that "new types of home ownership programs" will be explored in the model cities' endeavors.

Just how far HUD is able to take its intergovernmental responsibility will be watched with interest as the Department develops over the years. Now the HUD leadership role in problems affecting urban communities is based on the President's Executive Order on Coordination of Federal Urban Programs, which directs Secretary Weaver and his assistants to call on other federal agencies whose programs are concerned with the cities to meet in *ad hoc* working committees for common solutions.

A spokesman pointed out that Secretary Weaver meets weekly with heads of HEW, Interior, Labor, and the Office of Economic Opportunity and often has meetings with other Cabinet and agency heads whose activities mesh with HUD programs.

One HUD effort to establish more effective intergovernmental relations can be observed in the application of a program to give awards for "outstanding intergovernmental actions to improve living conditions in their areas." Selected from eighty-five submissions, the first Urban Development Intergovernmental Awards went to ten public bodies, ranging from Laramie, Wyoming, to the state of Georgia. The Laramie award recognized cooperation with the county school board in establishing an "education park" to carry out the school park segment of Laramie's general comprehensive plan. A joint program of acquisition and development of school and park sites was cited as an influence for the Wyoming Land and Water Conservation Commission to request funds to update its state lands to include a statewide program of development of joint park sites. The Georgia award recognized the formation of its State Area Planning and Development

Commission, wherein individual counties and cities grouped themselves, voluntarily, into seventeen regional planning commissions, virtually covering the state. Each commission has a permanent staff of planners and technicians who have been effective in coordinating and administering various federal aid programs.

Much of tomorrow's working reality in HUD is expected to be seen in the model cities program.

One of the keys to the eventual success of model cities will be the strength of the "City Demonstration Agency" specified within the new HUD guidelines for a program to set forth goals and the approaches for achieving them. The CDA will receive the planning funds to establish the administration machinery for coordinating planning activities of the various local agencies in the proposed model neighborhood or section of the city. The CDA can be the city or county government or any local public agency designated locally under HUD guidelines. Assistant HUD Secretary for Demonstration Cities and Intergovernmental Relations Taylor has said the CDA must have authority to work out agreements, establish priorities, and allocate resources among governmental and nongovernmental agencies involved in the model program. When a plan is developed and approved by HUD, the CDA becomes eligible for a grant to administer its model program and also a program incentive grant. Generally, the CDA is eligible for a grant not to exceed 80 per cent of the aggregate local contribution to all projects and activities related to the total federal programs that might include urban renewal, neighborhood centers, hospital construction, community action programs, manpower training, urban beautification, vocational education, adult basic education, assistance to the medically indigent, and a work training (Neighborhood Youth Corps) program. Even before this 1966 legislation was signed by the President, Congress had appropriated $10.25 million for planning grants through June, 1968, $70 million for urban mass transportation grants for fiscal 1968, and $750 million for urban renewal grants for fiscal 1968.

Only a few dozen veterans of FHA's early history remain in upper-level positions in HUD's Washington headquarters or at the seven regional offices throughout the nation, but all of them and scores of senior mortgage and banking and building executives recall that the simple instrumentality of the government guarantee of a home mortgage loan and a system of stabilization for building and loan associations contributed mightily to stemming the foreclosure crisis of the mid-1930's and helped to put the private housing market on an upswing that continued, with only minor retrogressions, through the years.

Therefore, they feel, both government and private industry may be expected to work closely together in a search for a central mortgage facility to provide a secondary market for all types of home financing that will assure long-term home loans at reasonable and fairly stable rates. They believe that this HUD-approved search will be joined by builders, manufacturers, and nonprofit groups.

Chief among the ways in which HUD may prove its worth, beyond modest goals, is by bringing to life a new means of slum rehabilitation through the use of low-interest loans to make home owners out of slum dwellers. It is hoped that such loans to give slum families a stake in their dwellings will come from private sources. (Pension funds are most often mentioned.)

Whether HUD and the Congress can produce enough new ideas and the money to make them work to assure a better physical environment for all Americans is the essential challenge. The idea may be a workable, new, central mortgage facility or it may be a national home ownership foundation, or extension of the model cities program, but whatever the vehicle, one requirement is that the poor must be given a chance to rebuild dilapidated and neglected homes or to acquire possession of new residences by the use of low-interest mortgages.

Certainly, Secretary Weaver is aware of this compelling goal. In his words:

The richest nation in the world, with the most advanced scientific and technological base, cannot continue to tolerate unsafe, drab, unclean, inefficient communities. In the next generation, we are destined to build homes, stores, shops, factories, schools, and facilities equal to all we have ever built before. In doing so we must assure for all citizens freedom of choice within the limits of their economic capabilities. And this freedom should, and can, expand greatly the economic capabilities of our disadvantaged citizens.

There are plans, and they are based on achievements.

In 1966, Secretary Weaver described one successful project:

Moving into a new home is not particularly an unusual event in the lives of thousands of American families. But this is not an ordinary occurrence; this is not an average American family. For the first time in their lives, the children of Mr. and Mrs. Eugene Sharpfish will be living in a house. The Sharpfishes are American Indians on the Rosebud Sioux Indian Reservation in South Central South Dakota. For the past months they have been living in makeshift quarters, including a tent, an abandoned automobile body, and a trailer. They'd still be living in the tent, but it burned down. We at HUD are especially pleased to have played a part in giving this family a home.

The Sharpfish home in the Spring Creek section of the reservation was the first of 375 scheduled to be erected there. The prefabricated unit was assembled by fellow tribesmen under skilled supervision as part of a self-help project. Furnishings were acquired from a Bureau of Indian Affairs school no longer in operation, itself an example of some achievement in cooperation among government agencies.

Designed to show how low-income families can build homes for themselves and others, the demonstration project is jointly sponsored by four federal agencies and the Tribal Council of the Rosebud Sioux Indians. A total of $1.7 million in grants for the project was made by HUD, the Department of Health, Education, and Welfare, the Department of the Interior, and the Office of Economic Opportunity.

Under its low-income housing demonstration program,

HUD is providing basic materials for construction of the houses, at a cost of $610,000. A grant of $642,000 from the Office of Economic Opportunity is paying for the training and labor involved in building the houses. The Public Health Service of the Department of Health, Education, and Welfare is providing water and sewage disposal facilities at a cost of $367,000. The Bureau of Indian Affairs of the Department of the Interior is supplying prefabrication plans, plus construction equipment valued at $100,840.

The prefabricated unit was developed by the Battelle Memorial Institute of Columbus, Ohio, a nonprofit corporation. The units contain 620 square feet of living space and will cost about $3,000 each. They can be improved and expanded as family income increases. All houses will be equipped with a stove or space heater and designed for future installation of electricity and running water. The Sharpfishes will pay a $10 down payment, plus a monthly rental of $5 for 5 years.

In cooperation with the Battelle Memorial Institute, the tribe chose Father Richard G. Pates of Rosebud, a Jesuit priest, to direct the entire housing undertaking. As part of the project, a plant has been set up on the reservation, presently staffed full time by twenty residents, who are learning carpentry, plumbing, glazing, roofing, and electrical wiring. After the components are produced, a designated family will put up a house on a selected site. When all 375 houses have been built, the plant will attempt to supply the surrounding area with prefabricated homes and components.

According to Father Pates, the families chose what seems an appropriate name for the new housing program. They have called it, in Sioux, "Anpo-wich-arpi."

In English, that means "Dawn of a New Day."

# Appendix I

## DEMONSTRATION CITIES AND METROPOLITAN DEVELOPMENT ACT OF 1966
### (Public Law 89-754)

---

### TITLE I—COMPREHENSIVE CITY DEMONSTRATION PROGRAMS

*Findings and Declaration of Purpose*

Sec. 101. The Congress hereby finds and declares that improving the quality of urban life is the most critical domestic problem facing the United States. The persistence of wide-spread urban slums and blight, the concentration of persons of low income in older urban areas, and the unmet needs for additional housing and community facilities and services arising from rapid expansion of our urban population have resulted in a marked deterioration in the quality of the environment and the lives of large numbers of our people while the Nation as a whole prospers.

The Congress further finds and declares that cities, of all sizes, do not have adequate resources to deal effectively with the critical problems facing them, and that Federal assistance in addition to that now authorized by the urban renewal program and other existing Federal grant-in-aid programs is essential to enable cities to plan, develop, and conduct programs to improve their physical environment, increase their supply of adequate housing for low and moderate-income people, and provide educational and social services vital to health and welfare.

The purposes of this title are to provide additional financial and technical assistance to enable cities of all sizes (with equal regard to the problems of small as well as large cities) to plan, develop, and carry out locally prepared and scheduled comprehensive city demonstration programs containing new and imaginative proposals to rebuild or revitalize large slum and blighted areas; to expand housing, job, and income opportunities; to reduce dependence on welfare payments; to improve educational facilities and programs; to combat disease and ill health; to reduce the incidence of crime and delinquency; to enhance recreational and cultural opportunities; to establish better access between homes and jobs; and generally to improve living conditions for the people who live in such areas, and to accomplish these objectives through the most effective and economical concentration and coordination of Federal, State, and local public and private efforts to improve the quality of urban life.

## Basic Authority

Sec. 102. The Secretary of Housing and Urban Development (hereinafter referred to as the "Secretary") is authorized to make grants and provide technical assistance, as provided by this title, to enable city demonstration agencies (as defined in Section 112(2)) to plan, develop, and carry out comprehensive city demonstration programs in accordance with the purposes of this title.

## Eligibility for Assistance

Sec. 103. (a) A comprehensive city demonstration program is eligible for assistance under sections 105 and 107 only if:

(1) physical and social problems in the area of the city covered by the program are such that a comprehensive city demonstration program is necessary to carry out the policy of the Congress as expressed in section 101;

(2) the program is of sufficient magnitude to make a substantial impact on the physical and social problems and to remove or arrest blight and decay in entire sections or neighborhoods; to contribute to the sound development of the entire city; to make marked progress in reducing social and educational disadvantages, ill health, underemployment, and enforced idleness; and to provide educational, health, and social services necessary to serve the poor and disadvantaged in the area, widespread citizen participation in the program, maximum opportunities for employing residents of the area in all phases of the program, and enlarged opportunities for work and training;

(3) the program, including rebuilding or restoration, will contribute to a well-balanced city with a substantial increase in the supply of standard housing of low and moderate cost, maximum opportunities in the choice of housing accommodations for all citizens of all income levels, adequate public facilities (including those needed for education, health and social services, transportation, and recreation), commercial facilities adequate to serve the residential areas, and ease of access between the residential areas and centers of employment;

(4) the various projects and activities to be undertaken in connection with such programs are scheduled to be initiated within a reasonably short period of time; adequate local resources are, or will be, available for the completion of the program as scheduled, and, in the carrying out of the program, the fullest utilization possible will be made of private initiative and enterprise; administrative machinery is available at the local level for carrying out the program on a consolidated and coordinated basis; substantive local laws, regulations, and other requirements are, or can be expected to be, consistent with the objectives of the program; there exists a relocation plan meeting the requirements of the regulations referred to in section 107; the local governing body has approved the program and, where appropriate, applications for assistance under the program; agencies whose cooperation is necessary to the success of the program have indicated their intent to furnish such cooperation; the program is consistent with comprehensive planning for the entire urban or metropolitan area; and the locality will maintain, during the period an approved comprehensive city demonstration program is being carried out, a level of aggregate expenditures for activities similar to those being assisted under this title which is not less than the level of aggregate expenditures for such activities prior to initiation of the comprehensive city demonstration program; and

(5) the program meets such additional requirements as the Secretary may establish to carry out the purposes of this title: *Provided,* That the authority of the Secretary under this paragraph shall not be used to impose criteria or establish requirements except those which are related and essential to the specific provisions of this title.

(b) In implementing this title the Secretary shall

(1) emphasize local initiative in the planning, development, and implementation of comprehensive city demonstration programs;

(2) insure, in conjunction with other appropriate Federal departments and agencies and at the direction of the President, maximum coordination of Federal assistance provided in connection with this title, prompt response to local initiative, and maximum flexibility in programing, consistent with the requirements of law and sound administrative practice; and

(3) encourage city demonstration agencies to (A) enhance neighborhoods by applying a high standard of design, (B) maintain, as appropriate, natural and historic sites and distinctive neighborhood characteristics, and (C) make maximum possible use of new and improved technology and design, including cost reduction techniques.

(c) The preparation of demonstration city programs should include to the maximum extent feasible (1) the performance of analyses that provide explicit and systematic comparisons of the costs and benefits, financial and otherwise, of alternative possible actions or courses of action designed to fulfill urban needs; and (2) the establishment of programing systems designed to assure effective use of such analyses by city demonstration agencies and by other government bodies.

(d) Nothing in this section shall authorize the Secretary to require (or condition the availability or amount of financial assistance authorized to be provided under this title upon) the adoption by any community of a program (1) by which pupils now resident in a school district not within the confines of the area covered by the city demonstration program shall be transferred to a school or school district including all or part of such area, or (2) by which pupils now resident in a school district within the confines of the area covered by the city demonstration program shall be transferred to a school or school district not including a part of such area.

*Financial Assistance for Planning Comprehensive*
*City Demonstration Programs*

Sec. 104. (a) The Secretary is authorized to make grants to, and to contract with, city demonstration agencies to pay 80 per centum of the costs of planning and developing comprehensive city demonstration programs.

(b) Financial assistance will be provided under this section only if (1) the application for such assistance has been approved by the local governing body of the city, and (2) the Secretary has determined that there exist (A) administrative machinery through which coordination of all related planning activities of local agencies can be achieved, and (B) evidence that necessary cooperation of agencies engaged in related local planning can be obtained.

## Financial Assistance for Approved Comprehensive City Demonstration Programs

Sec. 105. (a) The Secretary is authorized to approve comprehensive city demonstration programs if, after review of the plans, he determines that such plans satisfy the criteria for such programs set forth in section 103.

(b) The Secretary is authorized to make grants to, and to contract with, city demonstration agencies to pay 80 per centum of the cost of administering approved comprehensive city demonstration programs, but not the cost of administering any project or activity assisted under a Federal grant-in-aid program.

(c) To assist the city to carry out the projects or activities included within an approved comprehensive city demonstration program, the Secretary is authorized to make grants to the city demonstration agency of not to exceed 80 per centum of the aggregate amount of non-Federal contributions otherwise required to be made to all projects or activities assisted by Federal grant-in-aid programs (as defined in section 112(1)) which are carried out in connection with such demonstration program: *Provided,* That no Federal grant-in-aid program shall be considered to be carried out in connection with such demonstration program unless it is closely related to the physical and social problems in the area of the city covered by the program and unless it can reasonably be expected to have a noticeable effect upon such problems. The specific amount of any such grant shall take into account the number and intensity of the economic and social pressures in the sections or neighborhoods involved, such as those involving or resulting from population density, poverty levels, unemployment rate, public welfare participation, educational levels, health and disease characteristics, crime and delinquency rate, and degree of substandard and dilapidated housing. The amount of non-Federal contribution required for each project in a Federal grant-in-aid program shall be certified to the Secretary by the Federal department or agency (other than the Department of Housing and Urban Development) administering such program, and the Secretary shall accept such certification in computing the grants hereunder.

(d) Grant funds provided to assist projects and activities included within an approved comprehensive city demonstration program pursuant to subsection (c) of this section shall be made available to assist new and additional projects and activities not assisted under a Federal grant-in-aid program. To the extent such funds are not necessary to support fully such new and additional projects and activities, they may be used and credited as part or all of the required non-Federal contribution to projects or activities, assisted under a Federal grant-in-aid program, which are part of an approved comprehensive city demonstration program. Such grant funds, however, shall not be used—

(1) for the general administration of local governments; or

(2) to replace non-Federal contributions in any federally aided project or activity included in an approved comprehensive city demonstration program, if prior to the filing of an application for assistance under section 104 an agreement has been entered into with any Federal agency obligating such non-Federal contributions with respect to such project or activity.

## Technical Assistance

Sec. 106. The Secretary is authorized to undertake such activities as he determines to be desirable to provide, either directly or by contracts or other arrangements, technical assistance to city demonstration agencies to assist such agencies in planning, developing, and administering comprehensive city demonstration programs.

## Relocation Requirements and Payments

Sec. 107. (a) A comprehensive city demonstration program shall include a plan for the relocation of individuals, families, business concerns, and nonprofit organizations displaced or to be displaced in the carrying out of such program. The relocation plan shall be consistent with regulations prescribed by the Secretary to assure that (1) the provisions and procedures included in the plan meet relocation standards equivalent to those prescribed under section 105(c) of the Housing Act of 1949 with respect to urban renewal projects assisted under title I of that Act, and (2) relocation activities are coordinated to the maximum extent feasible with the increase in the supply of decent, safe, and sanitary housing for families and individuals of low or moderate income, as provided under the comprehensive city demonstration program, or otherwise, in order to best maintain the available supply of housing for all such families and individuals throughout the city.

(b) (1) To the extent not otherwise authorized under any Federal law, financial assistance extended to a city demonstration agency under section 105 shall include grants to cover the full cost of relocation payments, as herein defined. Such grants shall be in addition to other financial assistance extended to such agency under section 105.

(2) The term "relocation payments" means payments by a city demonstration agency to a displaced individual, family, business concern, or nonprofit organization which are made on such terms and conditions and subject to such limitations (to the extent applicable, but not including the date of displacement) as are provided for relocation payments, at the time such payments are approved, by section 114(b), (c), (d), and (e) of the Housing Act of 1949 with respect to projects assisted under title I thereof.

(c) Subsection (b) shall not be applicable with respect to any displacement occurring prior to the date of the enactment of this Act.

## Continued Availability of Federal Grant-in-Aid Program Funds

Sec. 108. Notwithstanding any other provision of law, unless hereafter enacted expressly in limitation of the provisions of this section, funds appropriated for a Federal grant-in-aid program which are reserved for any projects or activities assisted under such grant-in-aid program and undertaken in connection with an approved comprehensive city demonstration program shall remain available until expended.

## Consultation

Sec. 109. In carrying out the provisions of this title, including the issuance of regulations, the Secretary shall consult with other Federal departments and agencies administering Federal grant-in-aid programs. The Secretary shall consult with each Federal department and agency affected by each comprehensive city demonstration program before entering into a commitment to make grants for such program under section 105.

## Labor Standards

Sec. 110. (a) All laborers and mechanics employed by contractors or subcontractors in the construction, rehabilitation, alteration, or repair of projects which—

(1) are federally assisted in whole or in part under this title and (2) are not otherwise subject to section 212 of the National Housing Act, section 16(2) of the United States Housing Act of 1937, section 109 of the Housing Act of 1949, or any other provision of Federal law imposing labor standards on federally assisted construction,

shall be paid wages at rates not less than those prevailing on similar construction in the locality as determined by the Secretary of Labor in accordance with the Davis-Bacon Act, as amended (40 U.S.C. 276a—276a-5): *Provided,* That this section shall apply to the construction, rehabilitation, alteration, or repair of residential property only if such residential property is designed for residential use for eight or more families. No financial assistance shall be extended to any such projects unless adequate assurance is first obtained that these labor standards will be maintained upon the construction work.

(b) The Secretary of Labor shall have, with respect to the labor standards specified in subsection (a), the authority and functions set forth in Reorganization Plan Numbered 14 of 1950 (15 F.R. 3176; 64 Stat. 1267; 5 U.S.C. 133z-15), and section 2 of the Act of June 13, 1934, as amended (48 Stat. 948; 40 U.S.C. 276c), and the Contract Work Hours Standards Act (76 Stat. 357).

## Appropriations

Sec. 111. (a) There are authorized to be appropriated, for the purpose of financial assistance and administrative expenses under sections 104 and 106, not to exceed $12,000,000 for the fiscal year ending June 30, 1967, and not to exceed $12,000,000 for the fiscal year ending June 30, 1968.

(b) There are authorized to be appropriated, for the purpose of financial assistance and administrative expenses under sections 105, 106, and 107, not to exceed $400,000,000 for the fiscal year ending June, 1968, and not to exceed $500,000,000 for the fiscal year ending June 30, 1969.

(c) Appropriations authorized under this section shall remain available until expended.

## Definitions

Sec. 112. As used in this title—

(1) "Federal grant-in-aid program" means a program of Federal financial assistance other than loans and other than the assistance provided by this title.

(2) "City demonstration agency" means the city, the county, or any local public agency established or designated by the local governing body of such city or county to administer the comprehensive city demonstration program.

(3) "City" means any municipality (or two or more municipalities acting jointly) or any county or other public body (or two or more acting jointly) having general governmental powers.

(4) "Local" agencies include State agencies and instrumentalities providing services or resources to a city or locality, and "local" resources include those provided to a city or locality by a State or its agency or instrumentality.

## Grant Authority for Urban Renewal Projects which are Part of Approved Comprehensive City Demonstration Programs

Sec. 113. Section 103(b) of the Housing Act of 1949 is amended by inserting after the first sentence the following new sentence: "In addition to the authority to make grants provided in the first sentence of this subsection, the Secretary may contract to make grants under this title, on or after July 1, 1967, in an amount not to exceed $250,000,000: *Provided,* That the authority to contract to make grants provided by this sentence shall be exercised only with respect to an urban renewal project which is identified and scheduled to be carried out as one of the projects or activities included within an approved comprehensive city demonstration program assisted under the provisions of section 105(c) of the Demonstration Cities and Metropolitan Development Act of 1966."

*State Limit*

Sec. 114. Grants made under section 105 for projects in any one State shall not exceed in the aggregate 15 per centum of the aggregate amount of funds authorized to be appropriated under section 111.

# Appendix II

## FEDERAL GRANT-IN-AID PROGRAMS WITH LOCAL MATCHING REQUIREMENTS

### HUD

1. Urban Renewal
2. Neighborhood Facilities
3. Urban Mass Transit
4. Open Space Land
5. Urban Beautification
6. Water and Sewer Facilities
7. Community Renewal Program
8. Code Enforcement Program
9. Demolition of Unsafe Structures
10. Low-Rent Public Housing

### HEW

*Office of Education:*

1. National Teacher Corps
2. Library Services and Construction
3. Adult Basic Education
4. Guidance Testing and Counseling
5. College Work Study Program
6. Higher Education Facilities
7. Vocational Education
8. Vocational Work Study
9. Instruction in Critical Subjects, Humanities and the Arts
10. Training and Skill Development Programs

*Vocational Rehabilitation Administration:*
Vocational Rehabilitation Services and Facilities

*Public Health Service:*

1. Hospital and Medical Facilities Construction
2. Air Pollution Control
3. Community Mental Health Centers
4. Community Health Services
5. Comprehensive Public Health Services

*Welfare Administration:*

1. Aid to Families with Dependent Children
2. Child Welfare Services
3. Maternal and Child Health Services
4. Medical Assistance to the Aged
5. Aid to the Blind
6. Aid to the Disabled
7. Medical Assistance Program
8. Old Age Assistance
9. Work Experience and Training

## INTERIOR

1. Waste Treatment Works Construction
2. Outdoor Recreation Facilities

## AGRICULTURE

1. Food Stamp Program
2. School Lunch Program

## COMMERCE

1. Highway Planning and Construction
2. Public Works and Development Facilities Grants

## LABOR

1. Training and Skill Development Programs
2. Neighborhood Youth Corps

## OEO

1. Community Action Programs
2. Special Impact Programs

## JUSTICE

Law Enforcement Assistance Program

Other Federal programs do not have local matching requirements and would not be included in the base in calculating the supplemental grant. However, many of these programs would have impact on area problems and should be utilized as appropriate. These programs include VISTA volunteers, Job Corps, U.S. Employment Service, Education of Children of Low-Income Families, and Supplementary Education Centers and Services.

# Appendix III

## HUD REGIONAL OFFICES

The offices of the seven HUD regional directors are located as follows:

Region I: 346 Broadway, New York City 10013—serving Connecticut, Maine, Massachusetts, New Hampshire, New York, Rhode Island, and Vermont.

Region II: 728 Widener Building, Chestnut and Juniper Streets, Philadelphia, Pennsylvania 19107 (Delaware, District of Columbia, Maryland, New Jersey, Pennsylvania, Virginia, West Virginia).

Region III: 645 Peachtree—Seventh Building, Atlanta, Georgia 30323 (Alabama, Florida, Georgia, Kentucky, Mississippi, North Carolina, South Carolina, Tennessee).

Region IV: Room 1500, 360 North Michigan Avenue, Chicago, Illinois 60601 (Illinois, Indiana, Iowa, Michigan, Minnesota, Nebraska, North Dakota, Ohio, South Dakota, Wisconsin).

Region V: Federal Office Building, 819 Taylor Street, Room 13-A-01, Fort Worth, Texas 76102 (Arkansas, Colorado, Kansas, Louisiana, Missouri, New Mexico, Oklahoma, Texas).

Region VI: 450 Golden Gate Avenue, P.O. Box 36003, San Francisco, California 94102 (Arizona, California, Guam, Hawaii, Nevada, Southern Idaho, Utah, Wyoming). Area Office: 909 First Avenue, Seattle, Washington 98104 (Alaska, Montana, Northern Idaho, Oregon, Washington).

Region VII: Ponce de Leon Avenue and Bolivia Street, P.O. Box 1105, Hato Rey, Puerto Rico 00919 (Puerto Rico and the Virgin Islands).

DEPARTMENTAL FIELD OFFICES

★ Regional Headquarters (7)

◇ Area Office (1)

◆ Field Office (53)

● FHA Insuring Office (76)

⊗ FHA Service Office (16)

○ FHA Valuation Station (34)

■ FNMA Agency Office (5)

□ FNMA Sales Office (1)

BOUNDARIES
ocations

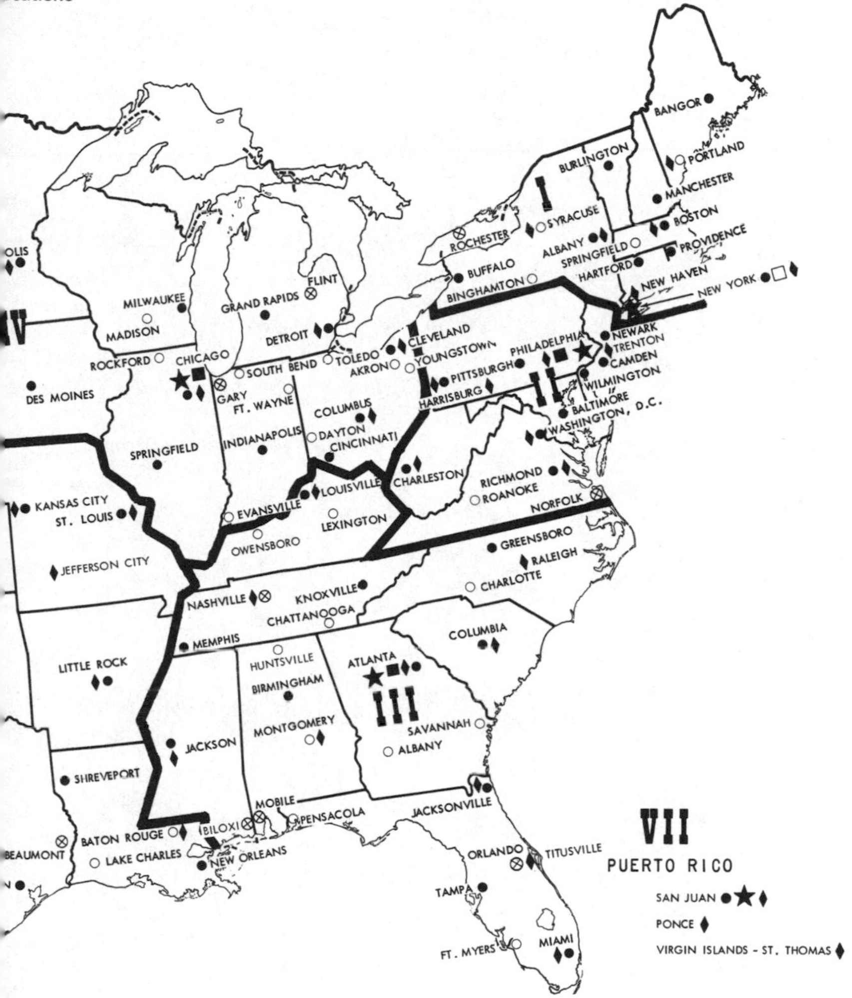

# Appendix IV

## FHA INSURING OFFICES

FHA insuring offices are located as follows:

ALABAMA, Birmingham; 2121 8th Avenue North 35203
ALASKA, Anchorage; Room 228, Federal Bldg. 99501
ARIZONA, Phoenix; 244 W. Osborne Road 13468
ARKANSAS, Little Rock; 3433 Federal Office Bldg. 72203
CALIFORNIA, Los Angeles; 5th & Broadway Bldg. 90013
  Sacramento; 1800-I Street 95809
  San Diego; 1415 Sixth Avenue 92101
  San Francisco; 100 California Street 94111
  Santa Ana; Freeway Center Bldg. 92701
COLORADO, Denver; Railway Exchange Bldg. 80202
CONNECTICUT, Hartford; Federal Office Bldg. 06103
DELAWARE, Wilmington; 536 Wilmington Trust Bldg. 19801
DISTRICT OF COLUMBIA; Railway Labor Bldg. 21412
FLORIDA, Coral Gables; 3001 Ponce de Leon Blvd. 33134
  Jacksonville; 21 West Church Street 32201
  Tampa; 4224-28 Henderson Blvd. 18165
GEORGIA, Atlanta; 230 Peachtree Street 30303
HAWAII, Honolulu; P.O. Box 3377 96801
IDAHO, Boise; 331 Idaho Street 83701
ILLINOIS, Chicago; 219 S. Dearborn Street 60604
  Springfield; 628 East Adams Street 62705
INDIANA, Indianapolis; Arch. & Builders Bldg. 333 Penn Street
  46209
IOWA, Des Moines; 615 Park Street 50309
KANSAS, Topeka; 700 Kansas Avenue 66603
KENTUCKY, Louisville; Madrid Bldg. 40202
LOUISIANA, New Orleans; Federal Bldg. 70113
  Shreveport; 627 Spring Street 71101.

MAINE, Bangor; Exchange Bldg. 04401
MARYLAND, Baltimore; 404 North Bond Street 21231
MASSACHUSETTS, Boston; 100 Boylston Street 02116
MICHIGAN, Detroit; 1249 Wash. Blvd. Book Bldg. 48226
    Grand Rapids; 921 Division Avenue North 49503
MINNESOTA, Minneapolis; 110 South Fourth Street 55401
MISSISSIPPI, Jackson; 301 Bldg. 39201
MISSOURI, Kansas City; 601 East 12th Street 64106
    St. Louis; 315 N. Seventh Street 63101
MONTANA, Helena; Steamboat Block 59601
NEBRASKA, Omaha; 215 North 17th Street 68102
NEVADA, Reno; 70 Linden Street 89505
NEW HAMPSHIRE, Manchester; P.O. Bldg., Hanover & Chestnut Streets 03105
NEW JERSEY, Camden; The Parkade Bldg. 08103
    Newark; 10 Commerce Court 07102
NEW MEXICO, Albuquerque; 625 Truman St. NE 87110
NEW YORK, Albany; City & County Savings Bank Bldg. 12207
    Buffalo; 304 U.S. Court House 14202
    Hempstead; 175 Fulton Avenue 11550
    New York; 2 Park Avenue 10016
NORTH CAROLINA, Greensboro; 221 South Ashe Street 27401
NORTH DAKOTA, Fargo; 700 Seventh Street South 58102
OHIO, Cincinnati; Federal Office Bldg. 45202
    Cleveland; 1375 Euclid Avenue 44115
    Columbus; Old P.O. Building 43215
OKLAHOMA, Oklahoma City; 1401 North Robinson 73103
    Tulsa; 9 East 4th Street Bldg. 74103
OREGON, Portland; Cascade Bldg. 97204
PENNSYLVANIA, Philadelphia; 2 Penn Center Plaza 19102
    Pittsburgh; 1000 Liberty Avenue 15222
PUERTO RICO, Santurce; Garraton Bldg. 00910
RHODE ISLAND, Providence; P.O. Annex 02903
SOUTH CAROLINA, Columbia; 1515 Lady Street 29201
SOUTH DAKOTA, Sioux Falls; 225 South Main Avenue 57102
TENNESSEE, Knoxville; 725 Gay Street S.W. 37902
TEXAS, Dallas; Wilson Bldg. 75201
    Fort Worth; 711 West Seventh Street 76102
    Houston; Rm. 7419 Federal Bldg. 77002

Lubbock; 1601 Ave. N. 79401

San Antonio; 535 South Main Avenue 78204

UTAH, Salt Lake City; P.O. Box 11009

VERMONT, Burlington; Federal Bldg., Elmwood Ave. 05402

VIRGINIA, Richmond; 400 N. Eighth Street 23240

WASHINGTON, Seattle; Norton Bldg., 801 Second Ave. 98104

Spokane; 501 American Legion Bldg. 99201

WEST VIRGINIA, Charleston; 500 Quarrier Street 25301

WISCONSIN, Milwaukee; 744 North 4th Street 53203

WYOMING, Casper; P.O. Box 580 82601

# Appendix V

## HUD'S MANPOWER NEEDS

A listing of the types of personnel required to administer effectively the programs of the Department of Housing and Urban Development reads like a dictionary of occupational titles. In total employment, HUD is one of the smallest of the federal departments, and yet it has a very large number of programs, which, although inter-related, are completely different in terms of the highly specialized types of personnel required. This problem is compounded by the fact that much of the manpower needed is in occupational areas that have come into being or experienced a major change in emphasis in the past decade. Therefore, in these fields there is no pool of experienced personnel from which to recruit.

Examples of a few new titles are: Director of Urban Studies, Community Development Advisor, Intergovernmental Specialist, Urban Economist, Demographer, and Demolition Consultant. The same types of personnel being recruited by HUD are also being sought by state and local governments, foundations, and universities, as well as private consulting and development firms. These circumstances have led to the realization that the recruitment effort needs to be rather heavily concentrated in four major groupings: (1) executive and top-level professional positions; (2) an intensive intern program for bringing in top-quality college graduate talent at the beginning level; (3) recruitment in several specific fields at the middle professional grades; and (4) secretarial recruitment.

To compensate for turnover, as well as to provide the additional staff required to carry out the new programs authorized both before and after the establishment of the Department, HUD will need to fill, in the aggregate, almost 1,800 professional, administrative, and managerial positions between now and June 30, 1968; it is estimated that approximately half will be filled by appointment of new employees. Roughly speaking, about 100 of the new appointments will be at the executive levels (GS-15 and above), about 500 at the intern levels of GS-5 through GS-9, and the remainder at the middle management levels.

The executive level positions fall into two major categories. First are the key administrative positions at the executive level which are concerned with urban program administration at the national or regional level. These positions require:

a background of responsible and successful experience of a broad and comprehensive nature at the federal, state or local level in program administration related to that with which the position is concerned (e.g., urban renewal, public works, etc.);

an understanding of intergovernmental relations and the ability to coordinate the activities of varied and sometimes highly divergent interests;

because of the many and significant interrelationships involved in the program, a substantial level of academic achievement is helpful for these positions;

because the programs are basically locality oriented, a substantial knowledge of local government operations is helpful.

Second are the executive level positions in such technical and professional areas as urban planning, engineering, architecture, real estate, urban sociology, taxation, municipal finance, zoning, urban technology, economics, law, program analysis and evaluation, management and budget analysis. These positions require:

genuine expertise in the subject matter involved and recognition among other professionals in the field of this expertise;

in addition, since in almost every instance these will be supervisory positions, administrative ability is required;

knowledge of local government operations is helpful.

The primary difference in requirements for the two types of key level positions described above is reversal in emphasis between subject matter expertise and administrative skill.

A preponderance of the positions at the middle levels are in the fields of construction inspection, real estate appraisal, and loan analysis. Candidates for these positions must have experience and training directly related to the work they will be doing:

The *Construction Representative* must have experience in the construction or inspection of construction of the type of structures being inspected, such as buildings or sewer and water systems.

The *Appraiser* must have responsible experience in the evaluation of property, which provides a thorough knowledge of the principles, methods, and practices of real estate appraisal and the ability to read plans and specifications and interpret legal documents.

The *Loan Specialist* must have experience in approval or disapproval of mortgage loans that involved analysis of the credit risk.

HUD hopes to fill many of its vacancies with experienced manpower, but is convinced it is neither possible nor desirable to fill all vacancies in this manner. In addition to the fact that there is keen competition for talent, sound personnel administration argues for the regular and continuing infusion of young people at the beginning levels. To provide this input, HUD administers its Housing Intern Program. Through this program, outstanding recent college graduates are selected for beginning level professional, technical, and managerial positions and given intensive on-the-job and formal training. Candidates selected for this program are assigned to such positions as Engineer, Urban Planner, Architect, Urban Renewal Representative, Metropolitan Development Representative, Finance Specialist, Loan Assistant, Attorney, Real Estate Advisor, Appraiser, Economist, Auditor, Market Analyst, Relocation Advisor, Housing Management Officer, Personnel Specialist, and many, many others.

Each of these positions has its own training requirements. For the engineering position, the candidate must have a degree in engineering, the architect a degree in architecture, the urban planner in urban planning, etc.

Generally, the college disciplines, in addition to the aforementioned, are: urban affairs, public administration, real estate, sociology, political science, law, finance, economics, business administration and accounting.

Candidates for the Intern Program, in addition to having a suitable educational background, must have a superior academic record, leadership ability as demonstrated by their extra-curricular activities in college, and the personal characteristics required for this program, such as ability to articulate, poise and presence, imagination, creativity, and drive.

In addition to the sizeable staffing problem in the technical professional and managerial levels, HUD has and will continue to have a need for able secretarial talent. Between now and the end of Fiscal '68, at least 450 typists and stenographers and secretaries need to be recruited.

Candidates for these positions must pass a Civil Service test and meet other Civil Service requirements for these positions.

Generally, candidates for these positions are high school or business school graduates or college graduates who have majored in secretarial science.

For secretarial positions, HUD seeks those with more and higher level experience.

Ability to effectively deal with the public and other officials of the Department is essential.

In summarizing HUD's manpower problems, it is clear that a difficult recruitment task lies ahead. This problem is recognized by HUD officials, and new efforts to solve the problem are in a developmental stage.

# Bibliography

The following books are suggested for additional reading in the field of housing and urban development:

ABRAMS, CHARLES. *The City Is the Frontier*. New York: Harper and Row, 1965.

———. *Man's Struggle for Shelter in an Urbanizing World*. Cambridge, Mass.: M.I.T. Press, 1964.

ANDERSON, MARTIN. *The Federal Bulldozer; A Critical Analysis of Urban Renewal, 1949–1962*. Cambridge, Mass.: M.I.T. Press, 1964.

BERGEL, EGON ERNEST. *Urban Sociology*. New York: McGraw-Hill Book Co., 1955.

BEYER, GLENN H. *Housing: A Factual Analysis*. New York: The Macmillan Co., 1958.

———. *Housing and Society*. New York: The Macmillan Co., 1965.

COLE, WILLIAM E. *Urban Society*. Boston: Houghton Mifflin Co., 1958.

CONANT, JAMES BRYANT. *Slums and Suburbs: A Commentary on Schools in Metropolitan Areas*. New York: McGraw-Hill Book Co., 1961.

CUNNINGHAM, JAMES V. *The Resurgent Neighborhood*. Notre Dame, Ind.: Fides Publishers, 1965.

DAVIES, PEARL JANET. *Real Estate in American History*. Washington, D.C.: Public Affairs Press, 1958.

DAVIES, RICHARD O. *Housing Reform During the Truman Administration*. Columbia, Mo.: University of Missouri Press, 1966.

DOXIADIS, CONSTANTINOS A. *Urban Renewal and the Future of the American City*. Chicago: Public Administration Service, 1966.

FISHER, ROBERT MOORE. *20 Years of Public Housing*. New York: Harper Brothers, 1959.

FUTTERMAN, ROBERT A. *The Future of Our Cities*. New York: Doubleday and Co., 1961.

GALLAGHER, JOHN R., and O'DONNELL, JOHN J. *Nonprofit Housing Under Section 221(d)(3) of National Housing Act*. Washington, D.C.: Urban America, 1966.

GOTTMAN, JEAN. *Megalopolis: The Urbanized Northeastern Seaboard of the United States*. New York: Twentieth Century Fund, 1961.

GOTTMAN, JEAN, and HARPER, ROBERT A. (eds.). *Metropolis on the Move: Geographers Look at Urban Sprawl*. New York: John Wiley, 1967.

GRUEN, VICTOR. *The Heart of Our Cities; the Urban Crisis: Diagnosis and Cure*. New York: Simon and Schuster, 1964.

HAAR, CHARLES M. *Federal Credit and Private Housing; the Mass Financing Dilemma.* New York: McGraw-Hill Book Co., 1960.

*The Housing Yearbook, 1966.* The National Housing Conference. New York: Abco Press, 1966.

JACOBS, JANE. *The Death and Life of Great American Cities.* New York: Random House, 1961.

LEE, ROSE HUM. *The City; Urbanism and Urbanization in Major World Regions.* Philadelphia: J. B. Lippincott Co., 1955.

LYND, ROBERT S., and LYND, HELEN M. *Middletown.* New York: Harcourt, Brace & World, 1959.

————. *Middletown in Transition: A Study in Cultural Conflicts.* New York: Harcourt, Brace & World, 1963.

MCKELVEY, BLAKE. *Urbanization of America, 1860–1915.* New Brunswick, N.J.: Rutgers University Press, 1963.

MAIER, HENRY W. *Challenge to the Cities; an Approach to a Theory of Urban Leadership.* New York: Random House, 1966.

MORRIS, JAMES. *Cities.* New York: Harcourt, Brace & World, 1964.

MUMFORD, LEWIS. *The City in History, Its Origins, Its Transformations, and Its Prospects.* New York: Harcourt, Brace & World, 1961.

————. *Culture of Cities.* New York: Harcourt, Brace & World, 1938.

MURRAY, ROBERT W., JR. *How to Buy the Right House at the Right Price.* New York: P. F. Collier, 1965.

PELL, CLAIBORNE. *Megalopolis Unbound; the Super-City and the Transportation of Tomorrow.* New York: Frederick A. Praeger, 1966.

ROCHE, JOHN P. *The Quest for the Dream; the Development of Civil Rights and Human Relations in Modern America.* New York: The Macmillan Co., 1963.

RODWIN, LLOYD (ed.). *Future Metropolis.* New York: George Braziller, 1960.

SCHLIVEK, LOUIS B. *Man in Metropolis.* Garden City, N.Y.: Doubleday and Co., 1965.

SPEIREGEN, PAUL D. *Urban Design: The Architecture of Towns and Cities.* New York: McGraw-Hill Book Co., 1965.

STRAUS, NATHAN. *Two-thirds of a Nation: A Housing Program.* New York: Alfred A. Knopf, 1952.

TILLY, CHARLES J. *Race and Residence in Wilmington, Delaware.* New York: Teachers College, Columbia University Press, 1965.

VON ECKARDT, WOLF. *The Challenge of Megalopolis; a Graphic Presentation of the Urbanized Northeastern Seaboard of the United States.* Based on the study of Jean Gottman. New York: The Macmillan Co., 1964.

WEAVER, ROBERT C. *Dilemmas of Urban America.* Cambridge, Mass.: Harvard University Press, 1965.

————. *Urban Complex: Essays on Urban Life and Human Values.* New York: Doubleday and Co., 1964.

WHALEN, RICHARD J. *A City Destroying Itself; an Angry View of New York.* New York: William Morrow, 1965.

WILLIAMS, OLIVER P. *Suburban Differences and Metropolitan Policies: A Philadelphia Story.* Philadelphia: University of Pennsylvania Press, 1965.

WOOD, ROBERT C. *1400 Governments: The Political Economy of the New York Metropolitan Region.* Cambridge, Mass.: Harvard University Press, 1961.

————. *Suburbia: Its People and Their Politics.* Boston: Houghton Mifflin Co., 1959.

## GOVERNMENT PUBLICATIONS

*Advance Acquisition of Land.* Washington, D.C.: HUD, June, 1966.

*Assistance for Urban Planning.* Washington, D.C.: Government Printing Office, June, 1966.

*Background and History 1938–1966.* Washington, D.C.: HUD, January 31, 1966.

"Beautification Aids for Urban Areas," Department of Housing and Urban Development *News,* Washington, D.C.: HUD, November, 1965.

*Federal Role in Urban Affairs.* Hearings before Senate Subcommittee on Executive Reorganization of the Committee on Government Operations, 89th Congress, 2d Session, December 30, 1966, Washington, D.C.: Government Printing Office, 1966.

*Housing and Urban Development Notes.* Washington, D.C.: HUD, December, 1966.

*HUD at a Glance.* Washington, D.C.: Government Printing Office, November, 1966.

HYMAN, LESTER S. *The Posture of the Department of Housing and Urban Development Toward the States.* Washington, D.C.: HUD, 1966.

*Information Circular Regarding the Activities of the Association.* Washington, D.C.: Federal National Mortgage Association, August 10, 1965.

*Metropolitan Social and Economic Disparities: Implications for Intergovernmental Relations in Central Cities and Suburbs.* U.S. Advisory Commission on Intergovernmental Relations. Washington, D.C.: Government Printing Office, 1965.

*Neighborhood Facilities Grant Program.* Housing and Home Finance Agency, Washington, D.C.: Government Printing Office, January 6, 1966.

*Programs of the Department of Housing and Urban Development.* Washington, D.C.: Government Printing Office, May, 1966.

*Rent Supplement Program.* Federal Housing Administration. Washington, D.C.: Government Printing Office, May, 1966.

*Secondary Market for Housing Mortgage.* Housing and Home Finance Agency. Washington, D.C.: Government Printing Office, 1965.

WEAVER, ROBERT C. *18th Annual Report of the Housing and Home Finance Agency, 1964.* Washington, D.C.: Government Printing Office, November, 1964.

————. *Secretary's Memorandum to the President on Organization.* Washington, D.C.: HUD, February 4, 1966.

*Years of Service to the Public and America's Housing and Home Finance Industry, 1938–1963.* Washington, D.C.: Federal National Mortgage Association, 1963.

## PERIODICALS

"Disaster," *The Journal of Housing,* Vol. 20 (July, 1966), pp. 396–398.

FALTERMAYER, EDMUND K. "We Can Cope With the Coming Suburban Explosion," *Fortune,* Vol. 74 (September, 1966), pp. 147–151.

"A Feverish New Push to Rehabilitate the Slums," *House and Home,* Vol. 31 (January, 1967), p. 18.

"FHA Takes Step to Take Funds from 221(d)(3)," *Realtor's Headlines,* Vol. 33 (October 3, 1966).

"48 Hour Rehabilitation," *Practical Builder,* Vol. 32 (June, 1966), p. 99.

"Housing a Nation," *Congressional Quarterly,* special annual report, 1966, p. 94.

"Instant Rehabilitation for Low-Income Families," *Journal of Homebuilding,* Vol. 20 (June, 1966), p. 42.

JONES, OLIVER H. "Wanted: A Federal Housing Policy," *The Mortgage Banker,* Vol. 26 (July, 1966), p. 22.

"Making American Cities More Livable," exclusive report and analysis presented with the Committee for Economic Development, *Saturday Review,* Vol. 49 (January 8, 1966), p. 120.

MILES, RUFUS E., JR. "The Case for a Federal Department of Education," *Public Administration Review,* Vol. 27 (March, 1967), pp. 1–9.

"New Attack on City Problems—How It Is To Work," *U.S. News & World Report,* Vol. 61 (October 31, 1966), p. 47.

"New Towns," *American Builder,* Vol. 99 (June, 1966), pp. 95–97. Comments by Larry Blackmon, Carl Feiss, and Robert C. Weaver.

"1966 Housing Legislation Starts Moving in Late June," *The Journal of Housing,* Vol. 20 (June, 1966), p. 310.

SCHALLER, LYLE E. "Church Sponsorship of Housing," *The Journal of Housing,* Vol. 20 (April, 1966), p. 195.

"Score on Housing Renewal Referenda: 16 Approvals, 10 Losses," *The Journal of Housing,* Vol. 20 (May, 1966), p. 273.

STEWART, CHARLES T. "Impact of Federal Policy on the Future City," *Realtor's Headlines,* Vol. 33 (April 4, 1966), p. 3.

WEAVER, ROBERT C. "Future Prospects in Housing Finance," *The Mortgage Banker,* Vol. 26 (December, 1966), p. 27.

"What HUD's Organization Means to Builders," *American Builder,* Vol. 100 (January, 1967), p. 8.

WOOD, ROBERT C. "A Creative Partnership Between Public Goals and Private Means," *The Mortgage Banker,* Vol. 26 (October, 1966), p. 28.

WORKMAN, ARNOLD. "Urban Development Stress for '67," *National Real Estate Investor,* Vol. 9 (January, 1967), pp. 48–51.

# Index